cupcakes!

by Elinor Klivans

photographs by France Ruffenach

CHRONICLE BOOKS
SAN FRANCISCO

Library of Congress Cataloging-in-Publication Data available.

ISBN 0-8118-4545-1

Manufactured in China.

Designed by Vanessa Dina
Prop styling by Sara Slavin
Food styling by Amy Nathan
Food styling assistance by Katie Christ & Nan Bullock
Typesetting by Janis Reed

The photographer wishes to thank Amy Nathan for her
beautiful work, and her husband, Warren, for letting us
use their home. Sara Slavin for a gracious and beautiful
touch. Katie Christ and Nan Bullock for all their hard
work and support. Cedric Glasier for his support, and
Vanessa Dina for her open mind and beautiful design.

Distributed in Canada by Raincoast Books
9050 Shaughnessy Street
Vancouver, British Columbia V6P 6E5

10 9 8 7 6 5 4 3 2 1

Chronicle Books LLC
85 Second Street
San Francisco, California 94105

www.chroniclebooks.com

acknowledgments

Judith Weber, my agent, who always leads me in the right direction. Bill LeBlond, my editor, who loved this idea from the very beginning. Amy Treadwell, assistant editor, who started it all and helped it to reach the fantastic finish.

A giant thank you to the rest of the brilliant publishing team at Chronicle Books.

Judith Sutton, my copy editor, who understood exactly how these cupcakes should speak.

France Ruffenach, whose photographs capture the "cupcake spirit."

Amy Nathan, my food stylist; Sara Slavin, my prop stylist; and food styling assistants Katie Christ and Nan Bullock, who made such a terrific team.

My husband, Jeff, who not only tasted every successful and not-so-successful cupcake but also became a cupcake baker along the way.

My daughter, Laura, who found time in her hectic life to proofread every recipe and offer her insightful advice to make the recipes better, and my son-in-law, Michael, whom I can always count on to give support (and taste a few cupcakes).

My son, Peter, who proofread every recipe, no matter where he was—home or on the other side of the world—and my daughter-in-law, Kate, who tested and baked and had a good time with it all.

My mother, who baked all of those birthday-party cupcakes, and, my father, who enjoyed it all.

Thank you to the cupcake testers who tested so many recipes: Jeffrey Klivans, Melissa McDaniel, Madison Olds, Dawn Ryan, Louise Shames, Kate Steinheimer, and Laura Williams.

A big thank you to my circle of supporters and encouragers: Melanie Barnard, Flo Braker, Sue Chase, Susan Derecskey, Susan Dunning, Natalie and Harvey Dworken, Carole and Woody Emanuel, Barbara Fairchild, Mutzi Frankel, Karen and Michael Good, Kat and Howard Grossman, Helen and Reg Hall, Carolyn and Ted Hoffman, Pam Jensen and Stephen Ross, Kristine Kidd, Alice and Norman Klivans, Dad Klivans, Susan Lasky, Robert Laurence, Rosie and Larry Levitan, Jeanne McManus, Gordon Paine, Joan and Graham Phaup, Janet and Alan Roberts, Louise and Erv Shames, Barbara and Max Steinheimer, Kathy Stiefel, Gail Venuto, Elaine and Wil Wolfson, Jeffrey Young, and the Wednesday Italian group, who thinks it is all *meraviglioso*.

dedication

For my favorite husband,
best daughter, and best son

CUPCAKES

and I have a long and happy history together.
One of my earliest memories is of carrying a plate of my
mother's Butter Cake Cupcakes with Sticky Fudge Frosting to
kindergarten for my birthday. And one of my most recent memories is
of just a few months ago when I baked chocolate cupcakes with my
granddaughter, Madison, to take to her kindergarten class for her
birthday. Then there were all those years in between
when I baked cupcakes to celebrate every birthday
and decorated cupcakes for every holiday. We carried them to picnics, potlucks, and countless bake
sales, and they were there to welcome the kids
home from school. An afternoon tea party called
for platters of bite-size tea cakes, and for dinner
parties, I brought out the showstopper versions.
I think you get the idea—cupcakes go anywhere,
at any time, and are for anybody. :: When this book
was just beginning to take shape and I was brainstorming with my editors, Bill LeBlond and Amy

Treadwell, the ideas literally started
pouring out. I began thinking out of the box,
or out of the cupcake liner, as it were. I knew at once   that
there would be upside-down cupcakes, cupcakes with fillings spilling out of their
sides, cupcakes with fillings hidden inside, tiny bite-size fudgy cupcakes, and
cupcakes covered in chocolate. As I baked what would in the end be about one
thousand cupcakes, the ideas kept coming, and I made cupcakes in ice cream
cones, cupcake ice cream sandwiches, and fluffy angel food and
chiffon cupcakes. Whenever company came for dinner, I put out
a platter of assorted cupcakes, with knives so friends could cut
them up and try them all. My children got into the act with
do-it-yourself cupcakes. They put out plates of plain cupcakes,
two flavors of frosting, and dishes of nuts, sprinkles, coconut,
chocolate chips, nonpareils, or whatever they had on hand.
Then grown-ups and kids had a ball spreading on frosting
(as much as they wanted) and adding their own toppings.
Inevitably it became a lively contest for the best-decorated
cupcake. :: When my daughter, Laura, made Chocolate-
Covered Brownie Ice Cream Cone Cupcakes for the first
time, she called them a recipe for happiness. That alone is
reason enough to start your ovens, put the frosting to the
cupcake, and have a cupcake—or maybe even two or three.

chapter 1:

MAKING GOOD CUPCAKES

• • •

• • •

"Keep it Simple" is the cupcake motto. Although cupcake and cake baking use the same general methods, cupcakes rely on straightforward and easy-to-understand preparations. Most recipes that make 12 to 18 cupcakes use about 1 cup of flour, which means about half the amount of batter that would be used for a large cake. These smaller quantities mix together quickly. Putting the frostings and toppings together is usually only an easy beating or stirring of ingredients. It's relaxed, informal baking.

Below I have provided general information about the supplies and ingredients used, mixing and baking methods, storage and transporting possibilities, and decorating ideas.

CUPCAKE SUPPLIES
Pans
Cupcakes are baked in muffin tins, and the terms "cupcake pan" and "muffin tin," or pan, are interchangeable. Cupcake history is sketchy, but the first cupcakes were probably created when someone decided to bake "cups" of cake batter in a muffin tin.

I prefer nonstick pans. If cupcakes are baked without paper liners or have tops that rise and bake onto the pan, they will release easily, and nonstick pans are certainly easier to clean. Cupcake pans come in three general sizes: regular, mini, and extra-large. The capacity of the cups for regular-size cupcakes can vary from 1/3 to 1/2 cup, and they come with either 6 or 12 cups per pan. Pans for mini-cupcakes, or tea cakes, have twelve 1-ounce cups in each pan. Pans for extra-large, or "Texas," cupcakes have cups with a 1-cup capacity and usually 6 cups per pan. To bake any of the recipes in this book, all you need are enough pans to bake 18 regular cupcakes, 48 mini-cupcakes, or 12 extra-large cupcakes. The pans are available in hardware stores, cookshops, and even supermarkets.

Many cupcake pans are dark in color. Usually I don't recommend dark pans because they absorb the heat so well that they can darken baked goods. But because cupcakes do not have a large proportion of sugar and the baking time is so short, the color of the pans doesn't seem to matter and dark and light-colored pans work equally well.

Pan Liners
The paper or foil liners, often labeled baking cups, for lining cupcake pans are standard supermarket items. These fluted liners come in a regular 2 1/2-inch size, a 1 5/8-inch mini-size, and a 3 1/2-inch extra-large size. Throughout the year, supermarkets and party stores display colorful paper liners with seasonal and holiday designs; I often buy these at a reduced price after the holiday has passed and save them for the next year. Paper or foil liners make for easy pan cleanup, keep baked cupcakes from drying out, and protect them when they are transported to a picnic or barbecue or during shipping.

Double Boilers

A heatproof bowl that will fit snugly over a pan of hot water, or a double boiler, is necessary for melting chocolate or beating a cooked egg white frosting. Use a non-reactive bowl, such as one of stainless steel or heatproof ceramic, that will not discolor white chocolate or react with acidic fruits.

Electric Mixers

You can use either a standing countertop electric mixer or a handheld electric mixer for any of these cupcakes and most of the frostings. Because the frosting for White Mountain Chocolate Cupcakes and Chocolate-Covered Hi-Hats must be beaten in a bowl over hot water, a handheld mixer is the best tool for these two recipes.

Miscellaneous Utensils

Graters are handy for grating citrus rind. Both Microplane graters and box graters work well. I prefer the Microplane graters that are patterned after a woodworker's rasp and make grating citrus rind a breeze. Have on hand several sets of measuring spoons, a set of dry measuring cups, and a liquid measuring cup. Dry measuring cups come in sets of four gradations and I recommend buying the stronger metal ones over the plastic ones. For liquids, use cups with clear markings and place the measuring cup on a flat surface when measuring. A 2-cup liquid measuring cup is a good general size to have. Rubber, or preferably heatproof silicone, spatulas in several sizes are useful for folding mixtures together and for scraping the last bit of batter or frosting from bowls. A strainer can do double duty as both a strainer for various mixtures or fruit purees and a sifter. For a regular flour sifter, I prefer one with a rotary handle.

Pastry Bags and Pastry Tips

A large pastry bag, about 16 inches long, is a good all-purpose size, but a heavy-weight resealable freezer bag can be substituted. Disposable plastic pastry bags are another good option. A large star tip and a large plain tip are the only ones needed for decorating these cupcakes.

Wire Racks

Most cupcakes are cooled on a wire rack. This allows for air circulation so the cupcakes do not get soggy on the bottom as they cool. Standard rectangular racks with thin cross-woven wires hold about a dozen cupcakes. It is useful to have two of these racks.

CUPCAKE INGREDIENTS

All the ingredients used for these cupcakes are readily available in supermarkets. Yes, you could send away for hazelnuts that are already peeled and toasted, but nowadays even supermarkets stock hazelnuts in some form. Speaking from experience, I recommend that you check the ingredients list before you bake to make sure that everything is on hand. Below are some brief notes about specific ingredients.

Butter and Oil

I use unsalted butter and corn or canola oil. I store butter in my freezer to keep it fresh. Be sure to taste or smell oils before using them to make sure they are fresh.

Chocolate

Check recipes ahead of time to see whether a recipe calls for unsweetened chocolate, semisweet chocolate, milk chocolate, white chocolate, or semisweet chocolate chips to make sure the right chocolate is on hand. Your results will be affected if you use one type of chocolate to replace another—except semisweet for bittersweet and vice versa.

Unsweetened and semisweet chocolate can be stored in a cool dark place, well wrapped, for up to 1 year. Because milk and white chocolate contain milk solids that can turn rancid, I wrap them well and store them in the freezer, for up to 3 months. Defrost the frozen chocolate in its wrapping, so any condensation forms on the wrapper, not on the chocolate. Semisweet chocolate chips can be stored in a cool dark place for up to 2 months, but milk and white chocolate chips should be used more promptly: 1 month in a cool dark place is the limit. All of these guidelines assume that the chocolate is fresh when purchased.

Citrus Zest

Citrus zest is the colored part of the rind of lemons, limes, and oranges. Rinse the fruit with warm water and dry it before grating the zest. Grate only the colored zest; the white pith underneath it is bitter. An average lemon or lime yields about 3 tablespoons of juice and 2 teaspoons of grated zest. A medium orange yields about 1/4 cup of juice and 2 to 3 teaspoons of zest.

Cream

Cream in cartons may be labeled whipping cream, heavy cream, or heavy whipping cream. Whipping cream has from 30 to 36 percent butterfat, and heavy cream and heavy whipping cream, which are the same, have from 36 to 40 percent. I used heavy whipping cream for these recipes. It whips firmer and holds up longer than regular whipping cream. Whipping cream can be substituted for heavy whipping cream, but the whipped cream—or chocolate sauce—will generally be slightly thinner.

An 8-ounce (1/2-pint) container of cream measures 1 cup and a 16-ounce (pint) container measures 2 cups.

Eggs

I use large eggs for all of my recipes. Eggs should always be stored in the refrigerator. Egg whites are usually separated from the yolks so that they can be whipped and the yolk and whites added separately to a recipe. It is easier to separate cold eggs. Since even a little yolk mixed in with egg whites will keep them from whipping (it is the fat in the yolk that interferes with the whipping), it is important to keep egg whites free of yolk. I crack eggs to separate the whites by breaking one egg white into a small bowl and transferring them one at a time to a large bowl. Then if a yolk breaks and mixes into the white, I have lost only one egg white. To separate egg yolks from egg whites, have ready a small bowl for the yolks, a small bowl to break one white at a time into, and a large bowl to hold all of the egg whites that will be used. Tap the eggshell on the thin edge of a bowl to make an even break on the eggshell about halfway around and pull the halves of the shell apart, keeping the yolk in one half of the shell (the yolk tends to cling to the shell) and letting the egg white drip into the small bowl. Drop the yolk into the other small bowl. Transfer the white to the large bowl and continue the process to separate as many eggs as you need. Egg whites left over from a recipe can be sealed tightly in a clean grease-free plastic container and frozen for up to 3 months; be sure to label the container with the date and the number of egg whites. Defrost the still-covered egg whites overnight in the refrigerator. Extra egg yolks should be used immediately or discarded.

Flavorings and Spices

Choose pure vanilla extract, made from vanilla beans, not artificial vanillin, and pure almond extract, which contains oil of bitter almond.

Store spices tightly covered, and replace stale ones. Spice storage times vary but should be measured in months, not years. You can check spices by tasting a tiny bit to make sure that they are fresh and have a good flavor. I use kosher salt, which is free of preservatives. It is slightly coarse, but it does pass through my flour sifter and strainer.

Flour

These recipes call for either unbleached all-purpose flour or cake flour. Cake flour is fine-textured and makes an especially light cupcake. Cake flour is usually sold in 2-pound boxes. The two common brands found in the baking section of most supermarkets come in bright red boxes that are easy to spot. I do not use self-rising cake flour.

Leavening Agents

Baking soda, or sodium bicarbonate, is an alkaline leavening that must be combined with an acid ingredient, such as sour cream, molasses, or buttermilk, to activate it. As soon as it is mixed into a batter, the baking soda is activated and the batter should be baked promptly. Stored airtight, baking soda keeps indefinitely.

I use double-acting baking powder, which is the most common type. Double-acting baking powder contains baking soda (alkaline) and two acid ingredients, one of which is activated by liquid and the other by heat. Batters that include double-acting baking powder do not have to be baked immediately, although this usually gives best results. Store baking powder tightly covered, and do not use it past the expiration date printed on the can.

Nuts

New crops of nuts appear in supermarkets from October to December, so autumn is a good time to buy a year's supply. I seal the nuts tightly in heavyweight freezer bags or plastic freezer containers and freeze them; it is easy to remove just what you need for a recipe. Defrost the nuts before baking with them, so they do not turn batters cold and thick.

Almonds and hazelnuts are often toasted before they are used. To toast them, spread the nuts in a single layer on a baking sheet and bake in a preheated 325°F oven for about 15 minutes, until they look evenly golden. Shake the pan once during baking to help them toast evenly, and check the nuts often at the end of the baking time to prevent burning. Toasting pecans and walnuts for about 5 minutes in a 325°F oven brings out their flavor.

Hazelnuts must have their bitter peel removed before they are used, so I recommend buying peeled hazelnuts. The King Arthur Flour Company (see Mail-Order Sources, page 141) ships them. To peel hazelnuts yourself, blanch the untoasted nuts in boiling water for 5 minutes, drain them in a strainer, and then immerse them in cold water for about 5 minutes to cool. Drain them again and use a small sharp knife to peel them. The skins slip off easily and the nuts are ready to toast. Any moisture will evaporate when the hazelnuts toast.

Sugar and Other Sweeteners

Store all sugars in tightly covered containers to keep them dry and free from insects. Brown sugar must be kept airtight. Corn syrup and molasses should be stored in the refrigerator to prevent any mold from forming. I use unsulphured molasses, which has not been processed with sulphur and has a milder flavor than sulphured molasses.

MIXING AND BAKING CUPCAKES

The time it takes to prepare the cupcakes and any frosting is listed at the beginning of these recipes. If the recipe includes another element, you should add that time to the "cupcake making" time. For example, White Mountain Chocolate Cupcakes use the Chocolate Sour Cream Cupcake Batter; the 10 minutes needed to prepare that batter should be added to the 20 minutes listed to bake the cupcakes, for a total of 30 minutes. The baking time and temperature are also listed for each recipe. Cupcakes lend themselves to being made in stages, and most can be baked one day and frosted or filled a day later.

When mixing a cupcake batter, it is important to know when you should beat the ingredients thoroughly and when you simply need to mix them together. Each recipe gives this information, of course, but I have summarized the general mixing methods below.

The Easy-Mix Yellow Cupcake Batter uses oil as its fat. For this type of batter, the eggs must be thoroughly beaten with the sugar to develop the cupcakes' texture. When the eggs and sugar are sufficiently beaten, the mixture will look thick and fluffy. It would be hard, in fact, to beat the batter too much at this stage. Once the eggs and sugar are thoroughly beaten, though, the purpose of additional mixing is to blend in the remaining ingredients just to incorporate them. Brownie-type batters also use a liquid fat, usually in the form of melted butter. These batters, which produce a dense, fudgy cupcake, only need to have their ingredients stirred together to blend them smoothly.

The Chocolate Sour Cream Cupcake Batter and Butter Cake Cupcakes with Sticky Fudge Frosting are both made with the type of batter that requires thorough beating of the butter and sugar plus additional beating when adding the eggs to develop the cupcakes' structure. The two beating steps incorporate air into the batter and help give the cupcakes a light texture. Then the remaining ingredients are just blended in.

The technique for making angel food cupcakes and chiffon cupcakes illustrates another type of mixing. Angel food cupcakes have no leavening and depend on well-beaten egg whites for their light texture. For chiffon cupcakes, well-beaten egg whites are gently mixed with a fluffy egg yolk mixture.

With the exception of cooked egg-white frostings, mixing frostings is usually simply a matter of beating the ingredients together until smooth. Old-fashioned marshmallow-like egg-white-and-sugar frostings, however, are beaten in a container set over a pan of hot water. They need to be cooked to the point that they increase in volume, become white and fluffy, and are firm enough to hold a shape.

For powdered sugar glazes, you just stir the liquid and dry ingredients together. The consistency of these glazes can be adjusted by adding a little more powdered sugar to thicken them or a little more of the liquid to thin them. For Chocolate Glaze made with hot cream, let it sit at room temperature (or in the refrigerator if time is short) until it cools to the desired consistency.

Filling Cupcake Pans

When filling pans or cupcake liners with batter, use a tablespoon or smaller spoon to drop the batter into the center of each cup or liner. Large mixing spoons make it difficult to fill them neatly. Rubber (or silicone) spatulas are useful for scraping all of the batter out of the bowl.

The size of the cupcake pan cups, of course, determines the cupcake size, but the quantity of batter used for each cupcake is also a factor. Use less batter, and the cupcake will rise just to the top of the liner or pan. Use more batter, and the cupcake forms a "big top" that rises over the top of the pan. These larger cupcakes are a nice choice when paired with a glaze or thin icing.

Most of these recipes take advantage of the convenience of paper liners. There are a few times, however, when I omit liners. I don't use them if I want the cupcake sides to be slightly crisp and lightly browned, or for upside-down cupcakes that have sticky bottoms that would stick to the liners, not the cupcakes. And angel food and chiffon cupcakes are baked without liners to allow the cupcakes to climb up the sides of the muffin cups.

When making either dense or very moist cupcakes, I spray the liners with nonstick spray. This keeps the baked cupcakes from sticking to the liners and prevents any large tops on cupcakes from separating from the cupcakes when you remove the liner. Nonstick spray makes it easy to coat the pleated sides of the liners.

I give the quantity of batter to use for each cupcake when filling the pans. If paper liners are used in the recipe, I also give a measurement for how high the batter should be in the liner. For regular paper liners, $1/4$ cup of batter will come to $1/2$ inch from the top, $1/3$ cup of batter will come to $1/4$ inch from the top, and a scant $1/2$ cup ($1/3$ cup plus 5 teaspoons) will fill the paper liner to the top. Once you've measured the batter for one or two cupcakes, you can visualize how much batter to use for the others.

Since paper liners help protect cupcakes from drying out and keep them stable during travel, I usually leave them on the cupcakes until I'm ready to serve them. Decorated paper liners can be left on the cupcakes for serving.

Baking Cupcakes

An average-size cupcake bakes for about 20 minutes—notice that the word "about" is included in every baking time. Baking times are general guidelines. Ovens vary, the temperatures of batters vary, and muffin tins vary, so check cupcakes often as the end of the baking time nears and use the touch and toothpick tests for them. Most cupcakes are done when the tops feel firm if lightly touched and a toothpick inserted in the center comes out dry. Exceptions include cupcakes with a melted chocolate center or lots of chocolate chips, and certain brownie-type cupcakes, which are underbaked for the desired results.

I bake cupcakes on the middle rack of the oven and seldom need to rotate the pans for even baking. When the oven rack is filled with several pans of cupcakes, the cupcakes may need several additional minutes to bake.

STORING AND FREEZING CUPCAKES

Most cupcakes can be covered and stored at room temperature or in the refrigerator for at least 2 days. Each recipe tells how that cupcake is best stored. Cupcakes without frosting can be wrapped tightly in plastic wrap, sealed in a container, and frozen for up to 2 months. With the exception of those that are frosted with a fluffy seven-minute frosting, a soft meringue, or whipped cream or are filled with pastry cream, most frosted or filled cupcakes can be frozen for up to 2 months. Frosted cupcakes must be chilled before they are wrapped so the frosting will firm up and not be squashed by the wrapping. Once the frosting is firm, wrap and seal them for the freezer. I wrap each cupcake in plastic wrap before sealing it in the clean container; wrapping them individually keeps them in top condition by protecting them from any air trapped in the container, and it makes it easy to take out as many cupcakes as you need. Leave the wrapping on while they defrost, so any moisture that forms will be on the wrapping, not on the cupcakes. Individually wrapped frozen cupcakes can go directly into lunch boxes or picnic baskets.

PORTABLE CUPCAKES

Cupcakes are designed to travel: most are handheld desserts that are already portioned out. To carry cupcakes to a friend, a party, or around the corner, pack them in a single layer in a sturdy box or plastic container.

The best cupcakes for shipping are ones that don't have soft frosting or fillings and that are normally kept at room temperature. Some good shippers here are Chocolate Chip Cupcakes, Orange Chiffon Cupcakes, Top-to-Bottom Crumb Cupcakes, Apple Streusel Cinnamon Swirl Cupcakes, Vanilla Cheesecake Crunch-Top Cupcakes, and Butter Almond Tea Cakes. After wrapping each cupcake in plastic wrap and sealing them in a container as described above, wrap packing material around the container and pack it in a larger carton with lots of packing material to cushion it. This protects it inside the carton and keeps it from being tossed around. Ship early in the week and send by a method that has the cupcakes arriving within 2 days, so they won't sit in a warehouse over the weekend.

DECORATING CUPCAKES

Crumb toppings or pineapple or pecan upside-down toppings bake with the cupcakes to make instant decorations, but frosted and glazed cupcake tops are palettes just waiting to be garnished. I prefer to use toppings that repeat the flavor or ingredients in a cupcake. Chocolate cupcakes could be finished with shaved chocolate, chocolate cutouts, or drizzles of melted chocolate, while the same dried fruits and nuts that are baked in Fruity, Nutty Harvest Cupcakes make a colorful topping. The tops of nut cupcakes can be rolled in chopped nuts to cover them completely, or the edges or centers, or entire tops, can be sprinkled with nuts. Whole nuts can be placed individually in the center of a cupcake or arranged as a border. Ginger- or citrus-flavored cupcakes look attractive topped with thin strips of candied ginger or citrus peel. Decorating cupcakes for a holiday calls for more of an anything-goes finish: colorful sprinkles, small candies, nonpareils, crushed peppermint candy—they all look festive.

chapter 2:

HEAD-START RECIPES

• • •

• • •

THE RECIPES FOR TWO CUPCAKE BATTERS, ONE FROST-
ING, AND TWO SAUCES INCLUDED HERE ARE USED
IN MANY DIFFERENT WAYS THROUGHOUT THE BOOK.
THEY ARE ALL SIMPLE AND THEY ARE ALL FAST. AFTER
MAKING ANY OF THEM ONCE OR TWICE, MIXING
BECOMES FAMILIAR AND TAKES EVEN LESS TIME.

The two basic cupcakes batters, one yellow and one chocolate, can be baked in a regular size, just right for topping with a mound of frosting, or they can be made as big-top cupcakes in a regular pan, with large tops for spreading with an even, rather than mounded, layer of frosting or icing. They can also be baked in pans that have large (Texas-size) openings to produce extra-large cupcakes, a type that often has a baked-on topping, or in mini-pans to make dainty mini-cupcakes or tea cakes. Many of the yellow cupcake recipes have nuts or fruit stirred into the bat-ter. And both the yellow and chocolate cup-cakes can be filled by scooping out the centers or slicing the cupcakes and adding filling between the cupcake layers.

• • •

The versatile vanilla cream cheese frosting can be flavored with orange or lemon zest or with cinnamon. White Christmas Cupcakes use a white chocolate variation of this cream cheese frosting.

• • •

The fudge sauce, filling, and glaze is used many times in each of those roles, and as the hot filling in Hot Chocolate Cupcakes. The chocolate sauce plus the yellow cupcake batter combine to make a light-chocolate-colored German Chocolate Cupcake. The lemon sauce and filling can be used to fill a gingerbread cupcake or coconut snowball, mixed with whipped cream to hold the "wings" of a butterfly cupcake, or spread under the meringue of a Lemon Meringue Cupcake.

• • •

The cupcake batters should be used as soon as they are mixed together. The sauces/fillings and the frosting can be made ahead and stored in the refrigerator or freezer.

easy-mix yellow cupcake batter

With this recipe I can have the batter for a moist yellow cupcake ready in minutes. Mixing the batter is a simple process of beating the eggs and sugar, then adding the liquids, sour cream, and dry ingredients. Using oil for the fat eliminates the step of softening butter. Beating the eggs and the sugar for a couple of minutes is the step that lightens the texture of the cupcakes, so don't skimp on that. Otherwise, it is all as easy as it sounds.

MIXING TIME : *about 5 minutes*

Batter for 12 regular cupcakes, 9 big-top cupcakes, 6 extra-large cupcakes, or 42 mini-cupcakes

1¼ cups unbleached all-purpose flour

½ teaspoon baking powder

¼ teaspoon baking soda

¼ teaspoon salt

1 large egg

1 large egg yolk

1 cup sugar

½ cup canola or corn oil

1 teaspoon vanilla extract

½ cup sour cream

Batter for 24 regular cupcakes, 18 big-top cupcakes, 12 extra-large cupcakes, or 72 mini-cupcakes

2½ cups unbleached all-purpose flour

1 teaspoon baking powder

½ teaspoon baking soda

½ teaspoon salt

3 large eggs

2 cups sugar

1 cup canola or corn oil

2 teaspoons vanilla extract

1 cup sour cream

Sift the flour, baking powder, baking soda, and salt into a medium bowl and set aside.

In a large bowl, using an electric mixer on medium speed, beat the egg and yolk (or eggs, for the larger quantity) and sugar until thickened and lightened to a cream color, about 2 minutes.

Stop the mixer and scrape the sides of the bowl as needed during mixing. On low speed, mix in the oil and vanilla until blended. Mix in the sour cream until no white streaks remain. Mix in the flour mixture until it is incorporated and the batter is smooth. The batter is ready to bake, or for additions such as nuts, fruit, or other flavorings.

:: chocolate sour cream cupcake batter ::

This batter produces a light, moist dark chocolate cupcake. As all good basic chocolate cupcakes should be, these are ready to be slathered with creamy fudge frosting. They can also be swirled with a mound of marshmallow-like frosting, covered with peppermint icing, or filled with a generous amount of chocolate mousse.

MIXING TIME : *about 10 minutes*

Makes enough batter for 18 regular cupcakes, 12 big-top cupcakes, 12 extra-large cupcakes, or 60 mini-cupcakes

3   ounces unsweetened chocolate, chopped

1   cup unbleached all-purpose flour

1/2   teaspoon baking powder

1/2   teaspoon baking soda

1/4   teaspoon salt

1/2   cup (1 stick) unsalted butter, at room temperature

1¼   cups sugar

2   large eggs

1   teaspoon vanilla extract

1/2   cup sour cream

1/2   cup water

Put the chocolate in a heatproof bowl or the top of a double boiler and place it over, but not touching, a saucepan of barely simmering water (or the bottom of the double boiler). Stir until the chocolate is melted and smooth. Remove from the water and set aside to cool slightly.

Sift the flour, baking powder, baking soda, and salt into a medium bowl and set aside.

In a large bowl, using an electric mixer on medium speed, beat the butter and sugar until smoothly blended and creamy, about 2 minutes. Stop the mixer and scrape the sides of the bowl as needed during mixing. On low speed, mix in the melted chocolate. On medium speed, add the eggs one at a time, mixing until each is blended into the batter. Add the vanilla and beat until the mixture looks creamy and the color has lightened slightly, about 1 minute. Mix in the sour cream until no white streaks remain. On low speed, add half of the flour mixture, mixing just to incorporate it. Mix in the water. Mix in the remaining flour mixture until it is incorporated and the batter looks smooth. The batter is ready to bake, or for additions such as nuts, fruit, chocolate chips, or other flavorings.

cream cheese frosting

Adding cream cheese to a powdered sugar frosting produces a not-too-sweet frosting that has a pleasant cream cheese flavor. It is soft, but it is firm enough to hold a shape and a good choice for piping designs and shapes on top of cupcakes. The basic vanilla-flavored frosting takes well to other flavors, including cinnamon, lemon or orange zest, or white chocolate. (See the individual cupcake recipes for exact measurements.)

This frosting is easiest to use when freshly made, but it can be stored in the refrigerator for 2 days, then brought to room temperature and beaten with an electric mixer until fluffy again.

Makes 3 cups

½ cup (1 stick) unsalted butter, at room temperature

6 ounces cream cheese, at room temperature

1 teaspoon vanilla extract

3 cups powdered sugar

In a large bowl, using an electric mixer on low speed, beat the butter, cream cheese, and vanilla until smooth and thoroughly blended, about 1 minute. Stop the mixer and scrape the sides of the bowl as needed during mixing.

Add the powdered sugar, mixing until smooth, about 1 minute, then beat on medium speed for 1 minute to lighten the frosting further. The frosting is ready to use, or for flavor additions.

:: chocolate fudge sauce, filling, and glaze ::

Hot fudge sauce, truffle filling, fudge frosting, or chocolate glaze—whatever you call this butter, cream, and chocolate combination, you are going to love it. It is easy, can be made ahead, and uses chocolate chips, which melt easily without any chopping. Making the sauce is as simple as heating cream and butter, then letting the chips melt in the hot cream. Stir in any flavorings and continue stirring (for just a few seconds) to make a smooth, thick chocolate sauce. That's it. To turn the sauce into a shiny glaze, you use 1/4 cup additional cream and heat some corn syrup with the cream and butter. The sauce or glaze can be refrigerated for up to 2 weeks and reheated as needed. The sauce can be made with regular whipping cream rather than heavy whipping cream, but it will be slightly thinner.

Makes about 1²/₃ cups sauce or a scant 2 cups glaze

SAUCE OR FILLING	GLAZE
3/4 cup heavy whipping cream	1 cup heavy whipping cream
2 tablespoons unsalted butter, cut into 2 pieces	2 tablespoons unsalted butter, cut into 2 pieces
9 ounces (1 1/2 cups) semisweet chocolate chips	3 tablespoons light corn syrup
1/2 teaspoon vanilla extract	9 ounces (1 1/2 cups) semisweet chocolate chips
	1/2 teaspoon vanilla extract

In a medium saucepan, heat the cream and butter (and corn syrup, if making the glaze) over low heat until the cream is hot and the butter has melted. The mixture should form tiny bubbles and measure about 175°F on a thermometer; do not let it boil. Remove the pan from the heat, add the chocolate chips, and let them sit in the hot cream for about 30 seconds to soften. Add the vanilla and whisk the sauce until it is smooth and all of the chocolate has melted.

You can use the sauce warm or let it sit at room temperature until it reaches the thickness desired. To store it, pour the cooled sauce into a small bowl, cover, and refrigerate for up to 2 weeks. Reheat as much sauce as is needed by spooning it into a saucepan and heating over low heat to soften or melt. For the glaze, let it sit at room temperature just until it is thick enough to spread.

CHOICES If you want to double either version of the recipe, use a large saucepan.

Add any flavorings after the chocolate melts; when the sauce is still warm, flavorings blend in easily. Flavoring options include: 1 to 2 tablespoons dark rum, brandy, Amaretto, Kahlua, or Grand Marnier; 1 ounce chopped unsweetened chocolate for a bittersweet chocolate sauce; 1 teaspoon grated orange zest (good with the orange liqueur, too); 1 teaspoon instant coffee dissolved in 1 tablespoon water (good with the Kahlua); or 1/4 teaspoon peppermint extract.

lemon sauce and filling

Lemon curd is a thick, smooth lemon butter sauce that can be used as a sauce, filling, or topping, or even mixed with whipped cream to make lemon cream. This sauce is inspired by lemon curd, but the classic recipe relies entirely on the eggs for thickening it and must be cooked very carefully to prevent curdling. My version breaks with tradition by adding cornstarch, which consistently produces a foolproof smooth sauce.

The sauce can be frozen for up to 3 months. It does not become rock-hard in the freezer, so you can easily spoon out the amount needed for each recipe and return the remainder to the freezer.

Makes 1 cup

1/4	cup (1/2 stick) unsalted butter	1	cup sugar
1/3	cup fresh lemon juice	2	tablespoons cornstarch, dissolved in 1/4 cup water
2	large eggs	1	teaspoon grated lemon zest
2	large egg yolks		

In a medium saucepan, heat the butter and lemon juice over medium heat until the butter melts and the mixture is hot, about 130°F on a thermometer.

Meanwhile, in a medium bowl, whisk the eggs, egg yolks, and sugar together to blend them, then whisk in the dissolved cornstarch. Whisking constantly, slowly pour the hot butter and lemon juice into the yolk mixture. Return the mixture to the saucepan and cook over medium heat, stirring constantly with a large spoon, just until it comes to a boil and thickens; it will take about 6 minutes. When thickened, the sauce will leave a path on the back of the spoon if you draw your finger across it and look clear rather than cloudy. Immediately remove from the heat, strain into a small bowl, and stir in the lemon zest. Press plastic wrap directly onto the surface of the sauce, use a toothpick to poke a few holes in the plastic wrap to let steam escape, and refrigerate until cold. The sauce will thicken further as it chills.

The sauce can be refrigerated for up to 3 days. Or, spoon the cold sauce into a plastic freezer container, leaving at least an inch of space in the top of the container, press plastic wrap onto the surface, seal tightly, and freeze for up to 3 months.

chapter 3:

CLASSIC CUPCAKES

• • •

• • •

"CLASSIC CUPCAKES"

MEANS TWO THINGS HERE.

First there are the familiar cupcakes that you found tucked in your lunch box, carried to bake sales, topped with candles for birthday parties, and gaily decorated for bridal showers: chocolate cupcakes with chocolate frosting, carrot and raisin cupcakes with orange cream cheese frosting, chocolate cupcakes with billows of white frosting, or yellow cupcakes with vanilla buttercream. Then there are original cupcake renditions of favorite cakes. Cloudlike Lemon Angel and Orange Chiffon Cupcakes, or Pineapple Upside-Down Cupcakes, or German Chocolate Cupcakes—new ideas inspired by classic cakes.

For an especially easy recipe, try the Kid-Simple Cupcakes, which are yellow with white frosting and ready to take part in any celebration. The kid-friendly frosting is a white "palette" that looks good with any type or color of decoration, and it is also firm enough to pipe from a pastry bag into fancy swirls. Other toppings include different frostings and glazes, fruit or nuts baked with the upside-down cupcakes, and chocolate chip, crumb, or cinnamon sugar toppings baked on top of the cupcakes. The brown sugar glaze that bakes on the fig cupcakes is also served as a sauce. :: Many of these toppings can be mixed-and-matched with other cupcakes. Chocolate Buttercream Frosting, Sticky Fudge Frosting, Milk Chocolate Glaze, or white frosting would fit well with any chocolate, vanilla, fudge marble, or chocolate chip cupcakes. Let your personal taste guide you.

:: white mountain chocolate cupcakes ::

Fluffy meringue-like seven-minute frosting forms snow-capped peaks on these dark chocolate cupcakes. The frosting is made by beating a sugar-and-egg-white mixture over hot water. You will need a handheld electric mixer for beating the frosting; it takes about seven minutes to increase in volume and become fluffy and firm enough to hold its shape. Although it takes time to beat and cook the frosting to its meringue consistency, the impressive, silken result is worth it.

Make the cupcakes. Position a rack in the middle of the oven. Preheat the oven to 350°F. Line 12 muffin tin cups with paper cupcake liners.

Fill each paper liner with a generous 1/3 cup of batter, to about 1/8 inch below the top of the liner. Bake just until the tops feel firm and a toothpick inserted in the center comes out clean, about 20 minutes. Cool the cupcakes for 10 minutes in the pan on a wire rack.

Use a small knife to loosen any tops that might have stuck to the top of the pan. Carefully place the wire rack on top of the cupcakes in their pan. Protecting your hands with pot holders and holding the pan and rack together, invert them to release the cupcakes onto the wire rack. Turn the cupcakes top side up to cool completely.

:: continued

MAKES 12 REGULAR CUPCAKES

CUPCAKE MAKING :
20 minutes

CUPCAKE BAKING :
350°F, for about 20 minutes

CUPCAKES

Chocolate Sour Cream Cupcake Batter for 12 big-top cupcakes (page 24)

SEVEN-MINUTE FROSTING

1¼ cups sugar

1/3 cup water

3 large egg whites

1/4 teaspoon cream of tartar

1 teaspoon vanilla extract

1/4 teaspoon almond extract

Make the frosting. Put the sugar, water, egg whites, and cream of tartar in a heatproof bowl or the top of a double boiler with at least a 2-quart capacity and beat with a handheld electric mixer on high speed until opaque, white, and foamy, about 1 minute. Put the bowl over, but not touching, a saucepan of barely simmering water (or the bottom of the double boiler). The top container should sit firmly over the pan of hot water; be sure to keep the cord of the electric mixer away from the burner. Beat on high speed until the frosting forms a soft peak that stands straight up if you stop the beaters and lift them up, about 7 minutes. The frosting should register 160°F on a thermometer. Remove the container of frosting from the water, add the vanilla and almond extracts, and continue beating for 2 minutes to further thicken the frosting.

Use a thin metal spatula to spread a thick layer of frosting, about ½ cup, over the top of each cupcake, dipping the spatula gently into the frosting to make swirls. Serve the cupcakes, or carefully cover them and refrigerate. Let sit at room temperature for about 20 minutes before serving.

The cupcakes can be refrigerated for up to 2 days.

:: kid-simple cupcakes ::

MAKES 12 REGULAR CUPCAKES

:::::::::::::::::::::::::::

CUPCAKE MAKING :

15 minutes

CUPCAKE BAKING :

350°F, for about 23 minutes

CUPCAKES

Easy-Mix Yellow Cupcake Batter for 12 regular cupcakes (page 23)

FROSTING

½ cup (1 stick) unsalted butter, at room temperature

3 cups powdered sugar

1 teaspoon vanilla extract

3 to 4 tablespoons whole milk

3 tablespoons colored sugar, nonpareils, sprinkles, candies, or finely chopped chocolate (optional)

Ready to play in the kitchen? All you need is this batter that mixes quickly before any kid gets impatient and a creamy white goofproof frosting to heap on top. Then add to the fun with a bunch of colorful sprinkles, sugars, nonpareils, or candies for decorating, and you have all of the ingredients for a happy birthday, jolly holiday, or any-time-of-the-year cupcake party.

I took a lead from my busy daughter and daughter-in-law for the frosting. When my daughter, Laura, was frosting cupcakes for her son's first birthday, I asked her what recipe she was using. She said, "The one on the box of powdered sugar." A few weeks later my daughter-in-law, Kate, was making cupcakes for her daughter's fifth birthday party, and I asked her what frosting recipe she was using. She said, "The one on the box of powdered sugar." Good enough for me. This frosting, adapted from the one on the box of powdered sugar, is ready to take on any decoration or to hold the birthday candles.

Make the cupcakes. Position a rack in the middle of the oven. Preheat the oven to 350°F. Line 12 muffin tin cups with paper cupcake liners.

Fill each paper liner with a scant ¼ cup of batter, to about ½ inch below the top of the liner. Bake just until the tops feel firm and a toothpick inserted in the center comes out clean, about 23 minutes. Cool the cupcakes for 10 minutes in the pan on a wire rack.

Carefully place the wire rack on top of the cupcakes in their pan. Protecting your hands with pot holders and holding the pan and rack together, invert them to release the cupcakes onto the wire rack. Turn the cupcakes top side up to cool completely.

Make the frosting. In a large bowl, using an electric mixer on low speed, beat the butter, powdered sugar, and vanilla together with 3 tablespoons milk, then add up to 1 tablespoon more milk if needed to form a creamy, smooth, spreadable frosting. Use a small metal spatula to spread about 2½ tablespoons of frosting over the top of each cupcake. Sprinkle the frosting lightly with colored sugar, nonpareils, sprinkles, candies, or finely chopped chocolate, if desired, holding each cupcake upside down and dipping just the frosted center or edges in the decorations to make a nice pattern.

The cupcakes can be covered and stored at room temperature for up to 2 days.

CHOICES The frosting can be flavored with ½ teaspoon almond extract or 1 teaspoon grated lemon or orange zest. Or, it can be divided among several bowls and each colored with a few drops (start with 1 drop) of food coloring. Use food coloring sparingly—you can always add another drop.

This recipe lends itself to doubling. Use the Easy-Mix Batter for 24 cupcakes and double the frosting ingredients.

:: chocolate chip cupcakes ::

CUPCAKES

2   cups unbleached all-purpose flour

2   cups packed light brown sugar

1   teaspoon baking soda

1/2 cup (1 stick) cold unsalted butter, cut into pieces

1   large egg

1   teaspoon vanilla extract

1   cup sour cream

1/4 cup whole milk

2   cups (12 ounces) semisweet chocolate chips

2/3 cup Chocolate Fudge Glaze (page 26), slightly warm

My mother's brown sugar chocolate chip cake can do just about anything. Although it started out as a square cake, I have used the recipe for brownies and for sandwich cookies, and now it has become a "stuffed with chocolate chips" cupcake. What always stays the same is the no-sifting-required, easy-mix batter, and the consistently good results.

Position a rack in the middle of the oven. Preheat the oven to 325°F. Line 18 muffin tin cups with paper cupcake liners.

Make the cupcakes. In a large bowl, using an electric mixer on low speed, mix the flour, brown sugar, and baking soda to blend them. Add the butter and mix until the butter pieces are the size of peas, about 2 minutes. You will still see some loose flour. Stop the mixer and scrape the sides of the bowl as needed during mixing. Mix in the egg and vanilla. The batter will still look dry. Mix in the sour cream and milk until the batter looks evenly moistened; you may still see some lumps of butter. Mix in the chocolate chips.

Fill each paper liner with about a generous 1/4 cup of batter, to about 1/3 inch from the top of the liner. Bake just until the tops feel firm and a toothpick inserted in the center comes out clean, about 25 minutes. If the toothpick penetrates a chocolate chip, test another spot. Cool the cupcakes for 10 minutes in the pans on wire racks.

Carefully place a wire rack on top of one pan of cupcakes. Protecting your hands with pot holders and holding the pan and rack together, invert them to release the cupcakes onto the wire rack. Turn the cupcakes top side up to cool completely. Repeat with the second pan of cupcakes.

Add the chocolate glaze. Use a fork to generously drizzle thin lines of the topping over each cupcake. Let the cupcakes sit at room temperature until the glaze is firm, or refrigerate the cupcakes for about 15 minutes to firm the topping quickly. Serve at room temperature.

The cupcakes can be covered and stored at room temperature for up to 2 days.

CHOICES Omit the chocolate topping and dust the cupcakes with powdered sugar.

:: chocolate cupcakes with chocolate buttercream frosting ::

MAKES 18 REGULAR CUPCAKES

:::::::::::::::::::::::::::

CUPCAKE MAKING :

20 minutes

CUPCAKE BAKING :

350°F, for about 20 minutes

CUPCAKES

Chocolate Sour Cream Cupcake
Batter for 18 regular cupcakes
(page 24)

FROSTING

3   ounces unsweetened chocolate,
     chopped

2 1/2 cups powdered sugar

1 1/2 tablespoons unsweetened
     Dutch-process cocoa powder

1 1/2 cups (3 sticks) unsalted butter,
     at room temperature

1   teaspoon vanilla extract

1/2 cup heavy whipping cream,
     at room temperature

Chocolate cupcakes with chocolate frosting are true cupcake classics, and these have a whole lot of creamy chocolate frosting topping each one. The secret to the exceptionally creamy texture is to beat it for several minutes after all of the ingredients are combined. If you forget to bring the whipping cream for the frosting to room temperature (as I often do), warm it briefly over low heat. These cupcakes are especially good with vanilla ice cream.

Make the cupcakes. Position a rack in the middle of the oven. Preheat the oven to 350°F. Line 18 muffin tin cups with paper cupcake liners.

Fill each paper liner with a generous 1/4 cup of batter, to about 1/3 inch from the top of the liner. Bake just until the tops feel firm and a toothpick inserted in the center comes out clean, about 20 minutes. Cool the cupcakes for 10 minutes in the pans on wire racks.

Carefully place a wire rack on top of one pan of cupcakes. Protecting your hands with pot holders and holding the pan and rack together, invert them to release the cupcakes onto the wire rack. Turn the cupcakes top side up to cool completely. Repeat with the second pan of cupcakes.

Make the frosting. Put the chocolate in a heatproof bowl or the top of a double boiler and place it over, but not touching, a saucepan of barely simmering water (or the bottom of the double boiler). Stir the chocolate until it is melted and smooth. Remove from the water and set aside to cool slightly.

Sift the powdered sugar and cocoa powder into a large bowl. Add the butter, and using an electric mixer on low speed, beat until smoothly blended, about 2 minutes. At first the mixture will look crumbly, but then it will form a smooth mass. Beat in the melted chocolate. Add the vanilla and cream, mixing to incorporate. On medium speed, beat the frosting for at least 3 minutes, until it looks smooth and creamy and the color lightens.

Using a small spatula, spread about 3 tablespoons of frosting on top of each cupcake, mounding the frosting in the center.

The cupcakes can be covered and stored at room temperature for up to 3 days.

CHOICES Remove the paper liners and serve each cupcake with a scoop of vanilla or your favorite flavor of ice cream.

:: german chocolate cupcakes ::

MAKES 12 REGULAR CUPCAKES

CUPCAKE MAKING :
25 minutes

CUPCAKE BAKING :
350°F, for about 23 minutes

CUPCAKES

Easy-Mix Yellow Cupcake Batter for 12 regular cupcakes (page 23), still in the large mixing bowl

1/2 cup **Chocolate Fudge Sauce (page 26), at a pourable consistency**

1/4 cup **semisweet chocolate chips**

Chocolate Fudge Sauce mixed with Easy-Mix Yellow Cupcake Batter produces a light-colored chocolate cupcake that is similar to a classic German chocolate cake. There is a nice chocolate chip surprise hiding under the generous layer of sticky pecan and coconut topping. These cupcakes should be stored in the refrigerator, but they are best brought to room temperature before they are served.

Make the cupcakes. Position a rack in the middle of the oven. Preheat the oven to 350°F. Line 12 muffin tin cups with paper cupcake liners.

Using a large spoon, stir the chocolate sauce into the batter until no light streaks remain. Fill each paper liner with 3 tablespoons of batter, to about 1/2 inch below the top of the liner.

Bake just until the tops feel firm and a toothpick inserted in the center comes out clean, about 23 minutes. Cool the cupcakes for 10 minutes in the pan on a wire rack.

Carefully place the wire rack on top of the cupcakes in their pan. Protecting your hands with pot holders and holding the pan and rack together, invert them to release the cupcakes onto the wire rack. Immediately turn the cupcakes top side up and sprinkle the chocolate chips over them, about 7 chocolate chips per cupcake. The chocolate chips will melt slightly on the warm cupcakes. Cool the cupcakes completely.

Make the frosting. In a medium saucepan, stir the half-and-half and butter over medium heat until the cream is hot and the butter has melted. A bit of steam will just begin to rise from the mixture; do not let it boil. In a large bowl, whisk the egg yolks, sugar, and salt until smooth. Whisking constantly, pour the hot mixture into the yolk mixture. Return it to the saucepan and cook over medium heat, stirring constantly, until the custard thickens and reaches 165°F on a thermometer; it should leave a path on the back of the spoon when you draw your finger across it. Remove the pan from the heat and strain into a medium bowl. Stir in the vanilla, coconut, and pecans.

Cover the frosting loosely and refrigerate until it is cool and thick enough to hold its shape on top of the cupcakes, about 1 hour.

Using a thin metal spatula, spread a generous 3 tablespoons of frosting on top of each cupcake, mounding it in the center. Serve, or cover and refrigerate. Let the cupcakes sit at room temperature for 20 minutes before serving.

The cupcakes can be refrigerated for up to 3 days.

FROSTING

1	cup half-and-half
6	tablespoons (3/4 stick) unsalted butter, cut into pieces
4	large egg yolks
3/4	cup sugar
1/8	teaspoon salt
1	teaspoon vanilla extract
1 1/2	cups (about 5 ounces) shredded sweetened coconut
1	cup (about 4 ounces) finely chopped pecans

:: fudge marble cupcakes ::

MAKES 12 REGULAR CUPCAKES

: :

CUPCAKE MAKING :

20 minutes

CUPCAKE BAKING :

350°F, for about 23 minutes

CUPCAKES

Easy-Mix Yellow Cupcake Batter for 12 regular cupcakes (page 23) still in the mixing bowl, 1/2 cup Chocolate Fudge Glaze (page 26), at a pourable consistency

FROSTING

3/4 **cup Chocolate Fudge Glaze (page 26), at room temperature**

One batch of Chocolate Fudge Glaze does double-cupcake duty here. Swirls of the warm glaze marble the cupcakes and then a layer of the glaze, cooled and thickened, frosts the top. The chocolate glaze is poured over the cupcake batter, but not mixed into it. The liquid glaze combines so easily with the batter that if the glaze and batter were stirred together, the cupcakes would become all chocolate rather than marbleized.

Make the cupcakes. Position a rack in the middle of the oven. Preheat the oven to 350°F. Line 12 muffin tin cups with paper cupcake liners.

Spoon 3/4 cup of the cupcake batter into a small bowl and set aside. Spoon the 1/2 cup chocolate glaze over the top of the batter in the large bowl; do not stir the glaze into the batter. Using a large spoon, scoop up both yellow batter and chocolate glaze for each cupcake and fill each paper liner with about 3 tablespoons. Spoon about 1 tablespoon of the reserved plain batter on top of each. The batter will be about 1/2 inch below the top of the liner.

Bake just until the tops feel firm and a toothpick inserted in the center comes out clean, about 23 minutes. Cool the cupcakes for 10 minutes in the pan on a wire rack.

Use a small knife to loosen any tops that might have stuck to the top of the pan. Carefully place the wire rack on top of the cupcakes in their pan. Protecting your hands with pot holders and holding the pan and rack together, invert them to release the cupcakes onto the wire rack. Turn the cupcakes top side up to cool completely.

Frost the cupcakes. Spread about 1 1/2 tablespoons of the chocolate glaze evenly over each cooled cupcake.

The cupcakes can be covered and stored at room temperature for up to 3 days.

mississippi mud cupcakes

The name tells the story here, as long as you know that "mud" stands for chocolate. Crushed chocolate sandwich cookies make the crunchy bottom, chocolate chips melt into the cupcake batter, and both crushed cookies and chocolate chips bake on top. It's good mud.

Position a rack in the middle of the oven. Preheat the oven to 350°F. Line 18 muffin tin cups with paper cupcake liners.

Spoon 1 tablespoon of the cookie pieces into the bottom of each paper liner, then spoon about 2 teaspoons of chocolate chips (about 8 chocolate chips) over the cookie pieces in each liner. Spoon a scant 1/4 cup of batter over the chocolate chips. Sprinkle the remaining chocolate chips and cookie pieces over the tops, pressing them gently into the batter.

Bake just until the tops feel firm and a toothpick inserted in the center comes out clean, about 22 minutes. Cool the cupcakes for 20 minutes in the pans on a wire rack.

Holding an edge of each cupcake liner, carefully lift the cupcakes from the pan and place them on a wire rack to cool completely. (Removing the cupcakes from the pan this way prevents the soft chocolate chips from getting squashed.)

Put the chopped chocolate in a heatproof bowl or the top of a double boiler and place it over, but not touching, a saucepan of barely simmering water (or the bottom of the double boiler). Stir until the chocolate is melted and smooth. Remove from the water and set aside to cool slightly.

Use a small spoon to drizzle thin lines of melted chocolate over the top of each cooled cupcake.

The cupcakes can be covered and stored at room temperature for up to 3 days.

MAKES 18 REGULAR CUPCAKES

CUPCAKE MAKING :
25 minutes

CUPCAKE BAKING :
350°F, for about 22 minutes

2 1/4 cups crushed chocolate sandwich cookies, such as Oreos, in 1/2- to 1/4-inch pieces (about 20 cookies)

1 cup (6 ounces) semisweet chocolate chips

Chocolate Sour Cream Cupcake Batter for 18 regular cupcakes (page 24)

3 ounces semisweet chocolate, chopped

:: peanut butter cupcakes with milk chocolate glaze ::

MAKES 12 REGULAR CUPCAKES

:::::::::::::::::::::::::::

CUPCAKE MAKING :

20 minutes

CUPCAKE BAKING :

350°F, for about 22 minutes

CUPCAKES

1	cup unbleached all-purpose flour
1	teaspoon baking powder
1/4	teaspoon salt
6	tablespoons (3/4 stick) unsalted butter, at room temperature
3/4	cup smooth peanut butter, at room temperature
1	cup packed dark brown sugar
1	large egg
1	teaspoon vanilla extract
1/2	cup milk (any fat content)

Peanut butter cups always remind me what a good match peanut butter and milk chocolate are. Here a hefty dose of peanut butter flavors the cupcake batter and milk chocolate the glaze for this cupcake version of the popular combination.

Make the cupcakes. Position a rack in the middle of the oven. Preheat the oven to 350°F. Line 12 muffin tin cups with paper cupcake liners.

Sift the flour, baking powder, and salt into a medium bowl and set aside.

In a large bowl, using an electric mixer on medium speed, beat the butter, peanut butter, and brown sugar until smoothly blended and lightened in color, about 1 minute. Stop the mixer and scrape the sides of the bowl as needed during mixing. Mix in the egg. Add the vanilla and beat for 1 minute, or until the batter is smooth. On low speed, add the flour mixture in 3 additions and the milk in 2 additions, beginning and ending with the flour mixture and mixing just until the flour is incorporated and the batter looks smooth.

Fill each paper liner with a generous 1/4 cup of batter, to about 1/3 inch below the top of the liner. Bake just until the tops feel firm and are lightly browned and a toothpick inserted in the center comes out clean, about 22 minutes. There will be a few small cracks on top. Cool the cupcakes for 10 minutes in the pan on a wire rack.

Carefully place the wire rack on top of the cupcakes in their pan. Protecting your hands with pot holders and holding the pan and rack together, invert them to release the cupcakes onto the wire rack. Turn the cupcakes top side up to cool completely.

Make the glaze. In a medium saucepan, heat the cream and butter over low heat until the cream is hot and the butter has melted. The mixture should form tiny bubbles and measure about 175°F on a thermometer; do not let it boil. Remove the pan from the heat, add the milk chocolate, and let it sit in the hot cream for about 30 seconds to soften. Add the vanilla and whisk the glaze until it is smooth and all of the chocolate has melted. (Return the glaze to low heat if necessary to melt the chocolate completely, whisking constantly.) The glaze should be thick enough to hold its shape when spread over the cupcakes. If it is too liquid to spread, let it sit at room temperature for 5 to 15 minutes, depending on the temperature of your kitchen.

Using a small spatula, spread 1 tablespoon of the glaze over the top of each cupcake.

The cupcakes can be covered and stored at room temperature for up to 3 days.

GLAZE

- ¼ cup heavy whipping cream
- 1 tablespoon unsalted butter
- 1 cup (about 5¾ ounces) chopped milk chocolate or milk chocolate chips
- ½ teaspoon vanilla extract

butter cake cupcakes with sticky fudge frosting

MAKES 12 REGULAR CUPCAKES

CUPCAKE MAKING :
25 minutes

CUPCAKE BAKING :
350°F, for about 22 minutes

These were the cupcakes that I would come home to after a "hard day" at school. Mom always frosted them with this ultra-smooth frosting, which uses condensed milk rather than powdered sugar to sweeten it. Once cool, it is a "stick to the roof of your mouth" fudge frosting, so be sure to spread it on the cupcakes as soon as it is made, when it is still slightly warm and easy to spread. Cake flour adds an especially tender texture to the butter cupcakes.

CUPCAKES

1¼ cups cake flour

1 teaspoon baking powder

1/8 teaspoon salt

1/2 cup (1 stick) unsalted butter, at room temperature

1 cup sugar

2 large eggs

1 teaspoon vanilla extract

1/2 cup whole milk

Make the cupcakes. Position a rack in the middle of the oven. Preheat the oven to 350°F. Line 12 muffin tin cups with paper cupcake liners.

Sift the cake flour, baking powder, and salt into a medium bowl and set aside. In a large bowl, using an electric mixer on medium speed, beat the butter and sugar until smoothly blended and creamy, about 2 minutes. Stop the mixer and scrape the sides of the bowl as needed during mixing. Add the eggs one at a time, mixing until each is blended into the batter. Add the vanilla and beat for 2 more minutes. On low speed, add the flour mixture in 3 additions and the milk in 2 additions, beginning and ending with the flour mixture and mixing just until the flour is incorporated and the batter looks smooth.

Fill each paper liner with 1/4 cup of batter, to about 1/2 inch below the top of the liner. Bake just until the tops feel firm and a toothpick inserted in the center comes out clean, about 22 minutes. Cool the cupcakes for 10 minutes in the pan on a wire rack.

Carefully place the wire rack on top of the cupcakes in their pan. Protecting your hands with pot holders and holding the pan and rack together, invert them to release the cupcakes onto the wire rack. Turn the cupcakes top side up to cool completely.

Make the frosting. Put the chocolate, butter, condensed milk, and salt in a heatproof bowl or the top of a double boiler and place it over, but not touching, a saucepan of barely simmering water (or the bottom of the double boiler). Cook, stirring constantly, until the chocolate and butter have melted and the frosting is smooth and thick, about 5 minutes. Remove from the water and stir in the vanilla.

Scrape the chocolate mixture into a large bowl and beat with an electric mixer at medium speed until the frosting thickens further and cools to lukewarm, about 2 minutes. When thickened, the beaters should form lines in the frosting. Frost the cupcakes immediately, using a small spatula to spread about 2 tablespoons of frosting on top of each one. Let the cupcakes sit uncovered until the frosting firms up, about 1 hour.

These cupcakes are best stored in a covered container to protect the frosting; store for up to 3 days at room temperature.

FROSTING

- **2 ounces unsweetened chocolate, chopped**
- **2 tablespoons unsalted butter, at room temperature**
- **1 14-ounce can sweetened condensed milk**
- **1/8 teaspoon salt**
- **1 teaspoon vanilla extract**

:: date and walnut cupcakes with orange cream cheese frosting ::

MAKES 12 REGULAR CUPCAKES

:::::::::::::::::::::::::::::

CUPCAKE MAKING :
20 minutes

CUPCAKE BAKING :
325°F, for about 25 minutes

Dark with brown sugar and cinnamon, studded with dates and walnuts, and slathered with soft frosting, these are cozy, winter-warming cupcakes.

Don't let the long ingredients list stop you—these cupcakes are well worth it!

Make the cupcakes. Position a rack in the middle of the oven. Preheat the oven to 325°F. Line 12 muffin tin cups with paper cupcake liners. Spray the inside of each liner with nonstick cooking spray.

Put the dates in a small bowl and pour the boiling water over them. Set aside to cool to room temperature, about 10 minutes.

Sift the flour, baking powder, baking soda, salt, and cinnamon into a medium bowl and set aside. In a large bowl, using an electric mixer on medium speed, beat the butter and brown sugar until smoothly blended and creamy, about 2 minutes. Stop the mixer and scrape the sides of the bowl as needed during mixing. Mix in the egg, molasses, and vanilla until blended. On low speed, add half of the flour mixture, mixing just to incorporate it. Mix in the buttermilk. Mix in the remaining flour mixture until it is incorporated and the batter looks smooth. Mix in the walnuts and dates, with any liquid that remains in the bowl.

CUPCAKES

1   cup (4 ounces) pitted dates, cut into approximately 1/2-inch pieces

1/2 cup boiling water

1 1/4 cups unbleached all-purpose flour

1/2 teaspoon baking powder

1/2 teaspoon baking soda

1/4 teaspoon salt

3/4 teaspoon ground cinnamon

1/4 cup (1/2 stick) unsalted butter, at room temperature

3/4 cup packed dark brown sugar

1   large egg

1   tablespoon unsulphured molasses

1   teaspoon vanilla extract

Fill each paper liner with 1/3 cup of batter, to about 1/4 inch below the top of the liner. Bake just until the tops feel firm and a toothpick inserted in the center comes out clean, about 25 minutes. Cool the cupcakes for 10 minutes in the pan on a wire rack.

Carefully place the wire rack on top of the cupcakes in their pan. Protecting your hands with pot holders and holding the pan and rack together, invert them to release the cupcakes onto the wire rack. Turn the cupcakes top side up to cool completely.

Frost the cupcakes. Use a large spoon to mix the orange zest into the frosting. Use a small spatula to spread about 1/4 cup of frosting on top of each cupcake, mounding the frosting to the center. Serve; or cover and refrigerate.

The cupcakes can be refrigerated for up to 3 days.

1/2 cup buttermilk (any fat content)
1   cup (4 ounces) coarsely chopped walnuts

FROSTING

2   teaspoons grated orange zest
1   recipe Cream Cheese Frosting (page 25), in a large bowl, at room temperature

:: lemon angel cupcakes ::

MAKES 9 LARGE CUPCAKES

::::::::::::::::::::::::::::::::::::

CUPCAKE MAKING :

20 minutes

CUPCAKE BAKING :

325°F, for about 35 minutes

CUPCAKES

1/2 cup cake flour

3/4 cup, plus 2 tablespoons sugar

3/4 cup egg whites (about 5 large)

1/2 teaspoon cream of tartar

1/8 teaspoon salt

1 1/2 teaspoons grated lemon zest

1/2 teaspoon vanilla extract

1/4 teaspoon pure almond extract

:: continued

An angel food cake batter produces cupcakes that look as if they could float away on one of the fluffy clouds they resemble. To produce these large cupcakes, scoop generous mounds of the meringue-like batter into each muffin cup. Angel food batter likes to climb up and cling to the sides of a pan, so don't be tempted to use paper liners for these cupcakes. The pan holds the cupcakes in place and keeps them from shrinking as they cool. Once they cool, these cupcakes are actually quite sturdy. Fresh fruit, especially berries, makes a nice accompaniment.

Make the cupcakes. Preheat the oven to 325°F. Have ready a muffin pan with 12 muffin cups. Put paper liners in 3 of the cups to protect the pan.

Sift the flour and 2 tablespoons of the sugar into a small bowl and set aside. In a large bowl, using an electric mixer on medium speed, beat the egg whites, cream of tartar, and salt until the whites are foamy and the cream of tartar dissolves. Beat on high speed until the egg whites look shiny and smooth and the beaters form lines in the mixture; if you stop the mixer and lift up the beaters, the whites should cling to the beaters. Slowly beat in the remaining 3/4 cup sugar, 2 tablespoons at a time, then beat for 1 minute. Mix in the lemon zest, vanilla, and almond extract. Beating on low speed, sprinkle 1/4 cup of the flour mixture over the egg white mixture at a time, beating after each addition to incorporate it.

Using about 1/2 cup for each, spoon the batter into the 9 unlined muffin cups. The batter may even be above the tops of the cups, but this stiff batter will not spill over the sides. Do not smooth the tops—let the batter remain in fluffy mounds. Bake for about 35 minutes, until the tops are golden and a toothpick inserted in the center comes out dry. The cupcakes will rise quite a bit.

:: continued

GLAZE

1	cup powdered sugar
1	tablespoon unsalted butter, melted
2	tablespoons plus about 1 teaspoon fresh lemon juice

Arrange 2 cans on a wire rack and invert the pan over the cans so the ends of the pan rest on the cans. This lets air circulate while the cupcakes cool upside down. Let cool completely, about 30 minutes.

Use a small knife to loosen the edges of the cupcakes from the pan. Carefully remove the cupcakes from the pan, using the knife to help release them if necessary, and set them right side up on the rack.

Make the glaze. In a small bowl, stir the powdered sugar and melted butter with enough lemon juice, beginning with 2 tablespoons, to make a smooth, pourable glaze.

Use a small spoon to drizzle the glaze over the top of each cupcake.

The cupcakes can be covered and stored at room temperature for up to 2 days.

:: sticky fig cupcakes with brown sugar glaze ::

It takes some pampering to make it happily through winter. So how about indulging in these large, moist cupcakes that bake with a brown sugar sauce, serving them with a pitcher of the warm sauce and a pitcher of cold cream? After all, it is winter.

Calimyrna or Black Mission figs work equally well for these cupcakes.

Make the sauce. In a medium saucepan, heat the butter, cream, and brown sugar over medium heat, stirring often, until the butter melts and the brown sugar dissolves. Increase the heat to medium-high, bring to a boil, and boil for 1 minute, stirring constantly. Remove from the heat and stir in the vanilla. Set aside.

Make the cupcakes. Position a rack in the middle of the oven. Preheat the oven to 350°F. Line 6 extra-large muffin tin cups with large paper cupcake liners. Spray the inside of each liner with nonstick cooking spray.

Put the water and figs in a small saucepan and bring to a boil; set aside to cool while you prepare the batter.

Sift the flour, baking powder, baking soda, and salt into a medium bowl and set aside. In a large bowl, using an electric mixer on medium speed, beat the butter and sugar until blended and creamy, about 2 minutes. Stop the mixer and scrape the sides of the bowl as needed during mixing. Add the eggs, lemon zest, and vanilla, mixing until smooth and thick. You may see a few small pieces of butter, which is fine. On low speed, mix in the flour mixture to incorporate it. Mix in the figs, with any liquid that remains in the pan.

:: continued

MAKES 6 EXTRA-LARGE CUPCAKES

:::::::::::::::::::::::::::::::

CUPCAKE MAKING :

20 minutes

CUPCAKE BAKING :

*350°F, for about 20 minutes;
then 225°F, for about 20 minutes*

SAUCE

2	tablespoons unsalted butter
1/2	cup heavy whipping cream
2/3	cup packed dark brown sugar
1	teaspoon vanilla extract

CUPCAKES

1	cup water
1	cup (about 4 ounces) dried figs, quartered
1 1/4	cups unbleached all-purpose flour
1	teaspoon baking powder
1/2	teaspoon baking soda
1/4	teaspoon salt

:: continued

Fill each paper liner with 1/2 cup of batter, to about 1/2 inch below the top of the liner. Bake until the tops feel firm and a toothpick inserted in the center comes out wet, about 20 minutes. Remove the pan from the oven and reduce the oven temperature to 225°F.

Spoon 1 tablespoon of the brown sugar sauce on top of each cupcake. The cupcakes will have risen to the top of the paper liners, so some sauce may drip down the sides onto the pan. Return the cupcakes to the oven and bake until a toothpick inserted in the center comes out dry, about 20 minutes. Cool the cupcakes for 10 minutes in the pan on a wire rack.

Carefully place the wire rack on top of the cupcakes in their pan. Protecting your hands with pot holders and holding the pan and rack together, invert them to release the cupcakes onto the wire rack, and turn the cupcakes top side up. If any sauce remains in the bottom of the pan, spoon it over the cupcakes. Let cool completely.

To serve the cupcakes, warm the remaining sauce over low heat. Remove the paper liners from the cupcakes and place each cupcake on a plate. Pass a pitcher of the warm sauce and another pitcher of cream to pour around or on top of the cupcakes.

The cupcakes can be covered and stored at room temperature for up to 3 days. The sauce can be made ahead, covered, and refrigerated for up to 5 days; warm before baking the cupcakes.

1/4 cup (1/2 stick) unsalted butter, at room temperature

3/4 cup sugar

2 large eggs

1 teaspoon grated lemon zest

1 teaspoon vanilla extract

Heavy whipping cream for serving

:: banana butterscotch cupcakes ::

CUPCAKES

1¼ cups unbleached all-purpose flour

½ teaspoon baking powder

½ teaspoon baking soda

¼ teaspoon salt

6 tablespoons (¾ stick) unsalted butter, at room temperature

1 cup sugar

2 medium bananas, broken into 1-inch pieces

2 large eggs

½ teaspoon vanilla extract

¼ cup buttermilk (any fat content)

1 cup (6 ounces) butterscotch chips

Butterscotch is right up there with fudge and caramel on my list of favorite flavors. This recipe has a double hit of butterscotch—banana cupcakes are studded with butterscotch chips and topped with a super-creamy, golden butterscotch frosting.

Make the cupcakes. Position a rack in the middle of the oven. Preheat the oven to 350°F. Line 12 muffin tin cups with paper cupcake liners.

Sift the flour, baking powder, baking soda, and salt into a medium bowl and set aside. In a large bowl, using an electric mixer on medium speed, beat the butter and sugar until blended and creamy, about 2 minutes. Stop the mixer and scrape the sides of the bowl as needed during mixing. Add the banana pieces, mixing until they are blended into the mixture; you will still see some small pieces of banana. Add the eggs one at a time, mixing until each is blended. Add the vanilla and beat for 1 minute. On low speed, add half of the flour mixture, mixing just to incorporate it. Mix in the buttermilk. Mix in the remaining flour mixture until it is incorporated and the batter looks smooth. Stir in the butterscotch chips.

Fill each paper liner with a scant ⅓ cup of batter, to about ¼ inch below the top of the liner. Bake until the tops feel firm and a toothpick inserted in the center comes out clean, about 25 minutes. Cool the cupcakes for 10 minutes in the pan on a wire rack.

Carefully place the wire rack on top of the cupcakes in their pan. Protecting your hands with pot holders and holding the pan and rack together, invert them to release the cupcakes onto the wire rack. Turn the cupcakes top side up to cool completely.

Meanwhile, make the frosting. In a medium saucepan, heat the half-and-half and brown sugar over low heat, stirring often, until the brown sugar melts. Increase the heat to medium-high, bring to a boil, and boil for 1 minute, stirring often. Pour into a small bowl and refrigerate until cool to the touch, about 45 minutes.

In a large bowl, beat the butter and powdered sugar with an electric mixer on low speed until smoothly blended, about 2 minutes. At first the mixture will look crumbly, but then it will form a smooth mass. Add the vanilla and brown sugar mixture and beat on medium speed until smooth and creamy, about 1 minute.

Use a small spatula to spread about 1½ tablespoons of frosting on top of each cupcake.

The cupcakes can be covered and stored at room temperature for up to 2 days.

FROSTING

- ¼ cup half-and-half
- ¾ cup packed light brown sugar
- ½ cup (1 stick) unsalted butter, at room temperature
- 1 cup powdered sugar
- ½ teaspoon vanilla extract

:: carrot, orange, and golden raisin cupcakes ::

Carrots may lend an air of goodness to these cupcakes, but their real job is to add their naturally sweet flavor and produce an exceptionally moist cupcake; the nutrition part is just a bonus. This is a moist batter that takes longer to bake than the usual cupcake. The orange cream cheese frosting is piped onto the cupcakes through a large plain pastry tip, covering the cupcake tops with an appealing thick spiral of frosting. Lemon zest is another option for flavoring the frosting.

Make the cupcakes. Position a rack in the middle of the oven. Preheat the oven to 325°F. Line 12 muffin tin cups with paper cupcake liners. Spray the paper liners with nonstick spray.

Sift the flour, baking soda, salt, and cinnamon into a medium bowl and set aside. In a large bowl, using an electric mixer on medium speed, beat the eggs and sugar until smooth and thick, about 1 minute. Stop the mixer and scrape the sides of the bowl as needed during mixing. On low speed, mix in the oil, vanilla, and orange zest until blended. Mix in the flour mixture to incorporate it. Mix in the carrots, raisins, and walnuts.

Fill each paper liner with 1/4 cup of batter, to about 1/2 inch below the top of the liner. Bake until the tops feel firm and a toothpick inserted in the center comes out clean, about 28 minutes.

Cool the cupcakes for 10 minutes in the pan on a wire rack.

Carefully place the wire rack on top of the cupcakes in their pan. Protecting your hands with pot holders and holding the pan and rack together, invert them to release the cupcakes onto the wire rack. Turn the cupcakes top side up to cool completely.

CUPCAKES

1	cup unbleached all-purpose flour
1	teaspoon baking soda
1/4	teaspoon salt
1	teaspoon ground cinnamon
2	large eggs
3/4	cup sugar
2/3	cup canola or corn oil
1	teaspoon vanilla extract
2	teaspoons grated orange zest
1	cup finely chopped or grated carrots (about 2 carrots)
3/4	cup golden raisins
1/2	cup (about 2 ounces) coarsely chopped walnuts

Frost the cupcakes. Use a large spoon to mix the orange zest into the frosting. Spoon the frosting into a large pastry bag fitted with a 1/4-inch plain pastry tip. Leaving about 1/4 inch of the edge of each cupcake plain, pipe a thick spiral of frosting to cover the top; the dark edge of the cupcake makes a nice contrast to the white frosting. Or, use a small spatula to spread about 1/4 cup of frosting on top of each cupcake, mounding the frosting in the center. Place a walnut half on top of each cupcake. Serve; or cover and refrigerate.

The cupcakes can be refrigerated for up to 3 days.

FROSTING

2 teaspoons grated orange zest

1 recipe Cream Cheese Frosting (page 25), in a large bowl, at room temperature

~~~~~~~~~~~~~~~~~~~~~~~

12 walnut halves

:: orange chiffon cupcakes with orange butter icing ::

MAKES 12 LARGE CUPCAKES

:::::::::::::::::::::::::::::::

CUPCAKE MAKING :

25 minutes

CUPCAKE BAKING :

325°F, for about 35 minutes

CUPCAKES

1½ cups cake flour

1   cup sugar

1   teaspoon baking powder

¼   teaspoon salt

⅓   cup canola or corn oil

4   large eggs, separated

⅓   cup water

1½ teaspoons grated orange zest

¼   cup fresh orange juice

1   teaspoon vanilla extract

½   teaspoon pure almond extract

¼   teaspoon cream of tartar

Chiffon cake was Harry Baker's famous but top-secret idea until he sold the recipe to General Mills in 1947. Baker's secret was to combine the qualities of a light angel food cake and a moist sponge cake in one cake and use oil to enrich the batter. The mixing is simply a matter of combining two fluffy mixtures, one of whipped egg whites and one of whipped egg yolks. As with the Lemon Angel Cupcakes, chiffon cupcakes like to climb up and cling to the sides of a pan, so do not use paper liners for these. You will need two large mixing bowls to prepare the batter.

Make the cupcakes. Preheat the oven to 325°F. Have ready a muffin pan with twelve ½-cup-capacity cups.

Sift the cake flour, ¾ cup of the sugar, the baking powder, and salt into a large bowl. Use a large spoon to make a well in the center of the flour mixture, and put the oil, egg yolks, water, orange zest, orange juice, and vanilla and almond extract in the well. Using an electric mixer on medium speed, beat the mixture until it is smooth and thick, about 3 minutes. Stop the mixer and scrape the sides of the bowl as needed during mixing. Set aside.

In another large bowl, with clean beaters, beat the egg whites and cream of tartar on medium speed until the whites are foamy and the cream of tartar dissolves. Beat on high speed until the egg whites look shiny and smooth and the beaters form lines in the mixture; if you stop the mixer and lift up the beaters, the whites should cling to the beaters. Slowly beat in the remaining ¼ cup of sugar, 1 tablespoon at a time, then beat for 1 minute. Stir about one-third of the beaten egg whites into the egg yolk mixture. Use a rubber spatula to fold in the remaining egg whites until no white streaks remain.

For easy pouring, transfer the batter to a pitcher with a lip. Using about ½ cup for each, pour the batter into the cups. The batter will come just to the top of each cup. Do not smooth the tops—let the batter remain in fluffy mounds. Bake for about 35 minutes, until the tops are golden and a toothpick inserted in the center comes out dry. The cupcakes will rise about ½ inch above the top of each cup.

Arrange 2 cans on a wire rack and invert the pan over the cans so the ends of the pan rest on the cans. This lets air circulate while the cupcakes cool upside down. Let cool completely, about 45 minutes.

Use a small knife to loosen the edges of the cupcakes from the pan. Carefully remove the cupcakes from the pan, using your fingers to gently rock them back and forth to help release them if necessary.

Make the icing. In a small bowl, stir the powdered sugar, melted butter, orange zest, and orange juice together until smooth and thick.

Use a small spatula to spread a thin layer of icing over the top of each cupcake, about 1 tablespoon for each.

The cupcakes can be covered and stored at room temperature for up to 2 days.

ICING

1½ cups powdered sugar

2 tablespoons unsalted butter, melted

1 teaspoon grated orange zest

3 tablespoons fresh orange juice

:: caramel-covered tea cakes ::

MAKES 42 MINI-CUPCAKES

::::::::::::::::::::::::::::::

CUPCAKE MAKING :

25 minutes

CUPCAKE BAKING :

350°F, for about 14 minutes

CUPCAKES

Easy-Mix Yellow Cupcake Batter for 42 mini-cupcakes (page 23)

FROSTING

1/2 cup (1 stick) unsalted butter

2 1/4 cups packed light brown sugar

1 5-ounce can (2/3 cup) evaporated milk

1/8 teaspoon salt

1 teaspoon vanilla extract

1/4 cup sour cream

I had just finished testing my cupcake recipes, or so I thought, when Betsy Perry told me about her Aunt Mary Gilliam's tea cakes with caramel frosting. Betsy said that her Aunt Mary uses a basic yellow cupcake recipe for the tea cakes, but that the frosting for them was "invented" by her aunt and has been enjoyed by three generations of the Gilliam family. A three-generation cupcake sounded as if I should get out my testing gear again. The frosting reminds me of old-fashioned penuche candy. Not only is it soft and creamy, but it has a fudge-like sugary quality. My husband, Jeff, liked it so much he commandeered the leftover frosting to spread on his morning toast. I'm just glad that I found out about this heirloom recipe in time to share it here.

You will need a candy thermometer to make the frosting. If you only have two mini-muffin pans, halve the recipe and make 24 cupcakes.

Make the cupcakes. Position a rack in the middle of the oven. Preheat the oven to 350°F. Line 4 mini-muffin tins with 12 cups each with mini–paper liners. (There will be 6 papers that are not filled with batter, but the liners protect the pan.) Spray 42 of the liners with nonstick spray.

Spoon a slightly rounded tablespoon of batter into each of the sprayed liners to about 1/4 inch below the top of the liner. Bake just until the tops feel firm, the edges have browned lightly, and a toothpick inserted in the center comes out clean, about 14 minutes. Cool the cupcakes for 5 minutes in the pans on wire racks.

Carefully place a wire rack on top of one pan of cupcakes. Protecting your hands with pot holders and holding the pan and rack together, invert them to release the cupcakes onto the wire rack. Turn the cupcakes top side up to cool completely. Repeat with the remaining cupcakes.

Make the frosting. Melt the butter in a large saucepan over medium heat. Stir in the brown sugar, evaporated milk, and salt, increase the heat to medium-high, and bring the mixture to a full boil that cannot be stirred down. Boil, stirring often with a wooden spoon, until the mixture measures 234°F on a candy thermometer, about 6 minutes. Immediately remove the pan from the heat and let the caramel sit for 5 minutes.

Meanwhile, remove the paper liners from the cupcakes.

Scrape the caramel into a large bowl, and whisk in the vanilla and sour cream. At first the caramel may seem firm and sugary, but as you keep whisking, it will become smooth and creamy. Spear the top of each cupcake with a fork and dip it in the warm frosting, covering the bottom and sides, then let any excess frosting drip back into the bowl and replace the cupcakes, top side down, on the wire rack. Let the cupcakes sit until the frosting is firm, about 30 minutes.

The cupcakes can be covered and stored at room temperature for up to 2 days. The frosting will lose some of its shine overnight, but it will remain soft and creamy.

:: cinnamon sugar puff cupcakes ::

MAKES 12 REGULAR CUPCAKES

CUPCAKE MAKING :

15 minutes

CUPCAKE BAKING :

350°F, for about 18 minutes

CUPCAKES

1½ cups unbleached all-purpose flour

1   teaspoon baking powder

½   teaspoon salt

¼   teaspoon ground nutmeg

6   tablespoons (3/4 stick) unsalted butter, at room temperature

½   cup sugar

1   large egg, lightly beaten

½   cup milk (any fat content)

COATING

6   tablespoons (3/4 stick) unsalted butter, melted

½   cup sugar

1¼ teaspoons ground cinnamon

My friend Carole Emanuel enjoys eating cupcakes more than baking them, so when she came across this recipe, she gave it to me to try. The medium-size cupcake puffs up in the center during baking. Rather than frosting, the tops of the cupcakes are rolled in melted butter and cinnamon sugar right after they are baked. That crunchy coating plus their light texture gives them the air of a doughnut. I prefer to bake these without paper liners. These cupcakes remove cleanly and easily from the pan, and without liners, their sides bake to a nice golden brown.

Make the cupcakes. Position a rack in the middle of the oven. Preheat the oven to 350°F. Spray the inside of 12 muffin tin cups with nonstick cooking spray.

Sift the flour, baking powder, salt, and nutmeg into a medium bowl and set aside. In a large bowl, using an electric mixer on medium speed, beat the butter and sugar until blended and creamy, about 1 minute. Stop the mixer and scrape the sides of the bowl as needed during mixing. Beat in the egg, mixing until smooth and thick. On low speed, add the flour mixture in 3 additions and the milk in two additions, beginning and ending with the flour mixture and mixing just until the flour is incorporated and the batter looks smooth.

Fill each muffin cup with about 3 tablespoons of batter, to about ½ inch below the top. Bake just until the tops feel firm and a toothpick inserted in the center comes out clean, about 18 minutes. Cool the cupcakes for 5 minutes in the pan on a wire rack.

Meanwhile, make the coating. Put the melted butter in a medium bowl. In another medium bowl, stir the sugar and cinnamon together.

Carefully place the wire rack on top of the cupcakes in their pan. Protecting your hands with pot holders and holding the pan and rack together, invert them to release the cupcakes onto the wire rack. Turn the cupcakes top side up and immediately roll them in the melted butter, then in the cinnamon sugar to coat it completely. Serve warm or at room temperature.

The cupcakes can be covered and stored at room temperature for up to 2 days.

apple streusel cinnamon swirl cupcakes

A ribbon of cinnamon sugar melts into the middle of this cupcake, then more cinnamon sugar makes a crisp topping. This batter has an especially easy mixing method. The dry ingredients are stirred together in a bowl, then the liquid ingredients and grated apple are simply stirred into them. Breakfast, coffee break, or teatime, all are good times for these cupcakes.

Position a rack in the middle of the oven. Preheat the oven to 350°F. Line 12 muffin tin cups with paper cupcake liners.

Make the swirl and topping. In a small bowl, stir the sugar and cinnamon together.

Make the cupcakes. In a small bowl, mix the grated apple and the 2 tablespoons cinnamon sugar together; set aside. In a large bowl, stir the flour, sugar, baking soda, and salt together. Make a well in the center of the flour mixture and add the eggs, oil, and vanilla, stirring until the ingredients are smoothly blended. Stir in the reserved apple mixture, with any juice that has been released.

Spoon about 2 tablespoons of batter into each paper liner. Sprinkle 1/2 teaspoon cinnamon sugar over the batter in each liner. Spoon the remaining batter over the cinnamon sugar, using a scant 2 tablespoons of batter for each cupcake. Use a pastry brush to dab the top of the batter with the melted butter. Sprinkle the remaining cinnamon sugar over the top.

Bake just until the tops are light brown and a toothpick inserted in the center comes out clean, about 25 minutes. Cool the cupcakes for 10 minutes in the pan on a wire rack.

Carefully place the wire rack on top of the cupcakes in their pan. Protecting your hands with pot holders and holding the pan and rack together, invert them to release the cupcakes onto the wire rack. Turn the cupcakes top side up to cool completely.

The cupcakes can be covered and stored at room temperature for up to 3 days.

MAKES 12 REGULAR CUPCAKES

CUPCAKE MAKING :
10 minutes

CUPCAKE BAKING :
350°F, for about 25 minutes

SWIRL AND TOPPING

1/2 cup sugar

2 teaspoons ground cinnamon

CUPCAKES

1 cup grated peeled apple (1 large apple)

2 tablespoons cinnamon sugar (from above)

1 1/4 cups unbleached all-purpose flour

3/4 cup sugar

3/4 teaspoon baking soda

1/4 teaspoon salt

2 large eggs

1 cup canola or corn oil

1 teaspoon vanilla extract

3 tablespoons unsalted butter, melted

:: classic cupcakes

sticky pecan upside-down cupcakes

These cupcakes need an extra-large muffin tin to hold all of their pecans, sticky topping, and batter. The glaze should stick to the cupcakes, rather than to paper liners, so I line the bottoms of the muffin tins with circles of wax paper. The pecan mixture bubbles up around the cupcakes and glazes the sides with a honey coating.

Position a rack in the middle of the oven. Preheat the oven to 350°F. Line the bottoms of 12 extra-large muffin tin cups with wax paper circles. Spray the inside of each cup and the paper circles with nonstick cooking spray.

Make the topping. In a medium saucepan, combine the butter, honey, and brown sugar and cook over medium heat, stirring constantly, until the butter and brown sugar melt and the mixture is smooth. Remove from the heat.

Make the cupcakes. Put 1½ tablespoons of the brown sugar syrup in the bottom of each muffin cup. Spoon 2 tablespoons of pecans on top of the syrup in each. Fill each one with about a generous ⅓ cup of batter, to just below the top of the pan.

Bake just until the tops feel firm and a toothpick inserted in the center comes out clean, about 25 minutes. (Insert the toothpick into the cupcake batter, not into the sticky pecan topping.) Cool the cupcakes for 2 minutes in the pan on a wire rack.

Use a small knife to loosen the cupcakes from the sides of the pan. Carefully place the wire rack on top of the cupcakes in their pan. Protecting your hands with pot holders and holding the pan and rack together, invert them to release the cupcakes onto the wire rack. Remove the paper circles. If any pecans should stick, replace them on the cupcakes. Leave the cupcakes pecan side up to cool. Serve warm or at room temperature.

The cupcakes can be covered and stored at room temperature for up to 2 days.

CHOICES Whipped cream or ice cream is a good serving option for these cupcakes.

TOPPING

½   cup (1 stick) unsalted butter

5   tablespoons honey

⅔   cup packed light brown sugar

1½ cups (about 6 ounces) pecans, coarsely chopped

CUPCAKES

Easy-Mix Yellow Cupcake Batter for 12 extra-large cupcakes (page 23)

pineapple upside-down cupcakes

These cupcakes turn an old-fashioned family favorite into dessert in a cupcake. Adding corn syrup to the brown sugar glaze guarantees a smooth glaze that doesn't separate or become grainy as it bakes. The pineapple topping eliminates any need for frosting, but a spoonful of whipped cream is always welcome.

Position a rack in the middle of the oven. Preheat the oven to 350°F. Line the bottoms of 12 extra-large muffin tin cups with wax paper circles. Spray the inside of each cup and the paper circles with nonstick cooking spray.

Make the topping. In a medium saucepan, combine the butter, corn syrup, and brown sugar and cook over medium heat, stirring constantly, until the butter and brown sugar melt and the mixture is smooth. Remove from the heat.

Make the cupcakes. Put 1 tablespoon plus 1 teaspoon of the brown sugar glaze in the bottom of each muffin cup. Put a slice of pineapple on the brown sugar glaze in each cup. Spoon a generous 1/3 cup of batter over each pineapple slice; the batter will come just to the top of each cup.

Bake just until the tops feel firm and a toothpick inserted in the center comes out clean, about 25 minutes. (Insert the toothpick into the cupcake batter, not into the pineapple.) Cool the cupcakes for 5 minutes in the pan on a wire rack.

PINEAPPLE TOPPING

6   tablespoons (3/4 stick) unsalted butter

2   tablespoons light corn syrup

1   cup packed dark brown sugar

12 pineapple slices (one 20-ounce and one 8-ounce can pineapple in its own juice), drained

CUPCAKES

Easy-Mix Yellow Cupcake Batter for 12 extra-large cupcakes (page 23)

WHIPPED CREAM TOPPING (optional)

1   cup heavy whipping cream

1   tablespoon powdered sugar

1/2 teaspoon vanilla extract

Use a small knife to loosen any tops that might have stuck to the pan. Carefully place the wire rack on top of the cupcakes in their pan. Protecting your hands with pot holders and holding the pan and rack together, invert them to release the cupcakes onto the wire rack. Leave the cupcakes upside-down to cool completely.

Make the whipped cream, if using. In a large bowl, using an electric mixer on medium-high speed, beat the cream, powdered sugar, and vanilla until firm peaks form.

Serve each cupcake topped with a large spoonful of whipped cream, if desired.

Without the whipped cream topping, the cupcakes can be covered and stored at room temperature for up to 2 days. Make the whipped cream just before serving the cupcakes.

:: top-to-bottom crumb cupcakes ::

MAKES 18 REGULAR CUPCAKES
:::::::::::::::::::::::::::::::::

CUPCAKE MAKING :
20 minutes

CUPCAKE BAKING :
350°F. for about 25 minutes

CRUMB BOTTOM AND TOPPING

1¼ cups unbleached all-purpose flour

1 cup packed light brown sugar

2 teaspoons ground cinnamon

¼ teaspoon salt

¾ cup (1½ sticks) cold unsalted butter, cut into pieces

CUPCAKES

Easy-Mix Yellow Cupcake Batter for 18 medium cupcakes (page 23)

Powdered sugar for dusting

My family often teases me about my efforts to load crumb-topped desserts with extraordinary quantities of crumbs. My latest idea surrounds a cupcake with crumbs. It has crumbs on the bottom, and crumbs on the top, and a bit of yellow cupcake in the middle: the ratio of crumbs to batter is about three to two. The family doesn't tease me at all about these cupcakes— it's hard to talk with your mouth full.

Position a rack in the middle of the oven. Preheat the oven to 350°F. Line 18 muffin tin cups with paper cupcake liners.

Make the topping. In a large bowl, stir the flour, brown sugar, cinnamon, and salt together, breaking up any large pieces of brown sugar. Add the butter. Using the paddle attachment of an electric mixer on low speed, a pastry blender, or your fingertips, mix the ingredients together until crumbs form; the largest crumbs should be about ½ inch in size.

Make the cupcakes. Spoon about 1½ tablespoons of the crumbs into the bottom of each paper liner. Spoon about 2½ tablespoons of batter into each liner. Spoon the remaining crumbs over the cupcakes, using about 1½ tablespoons for each; the crumb topping will come to about ⅜ inch from the top of the liner.

Bake just until the tops feel firm and a toothpick inserted in the center comes out clean, about 25 minutes. Cool the cupcakes for 10 minutes in the pans on wire racks.

Carefully place a wire rack on top of one pan of cupcakes. Protecting your hands with pot holders and holding the pan and rack together, invert them to release the cupcakes onto the wire rack. Turn the cupcakes top side up to cool completely. Repeat with the second pan of cupcakes.

Dust the tops of the cupcakes with powdered sugar before serving.

The cupcakes can be covered and stored at room temperature for up to 3 days.

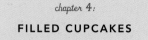

chapter 4:

FILLED CUPCAKES

· · ·

· · ·

FILLED CUPCAKES

ARE THE SANDWICHES OF THE CUPCAKE WORLD. THESE FILLINGS, SOMETIMES HIDDEN, SOMETIMES VERY VISIBLE, PUT THEM IN THE SUPER-SCRUMPTIOUS CATEGORY. THERE'S LEMON FILLING HIDING IN A COCONUT-COVERED SNOWBALL CUPCAKE, CHOCO-LATE MOUSSE SQUISHING OUT OF THE MIDDLE OF A CHOCOLATE CUPCAKE, AND AN ALMOST INVISIBLE CUPCAKE BURIED UNDER A MOUND OF FRESH STRAWBERRIES AND SOFT WHIPPED CREAM.

There are a lot of ways to fill a cupcake, whether it's a surprise filling in the middle of a cupcake, a layer showing through the edges of a split cupcake, or an abundant filling that is very much in plain view. To fill the centers of baked cupcakes, such as Gingerbread Cupcakes with Lemon Filling, I cut out a piece from the top of each cupcake, usually cone-shaped, and fill the hole. Depending on the finishing touch, these pieces of cupcake are replaced or discarded. Hot Chocolate Cupcakes have a chocolate sauce filling baked with the cupcakes, and Vanilla Cheesecake Crunch-Top Cupcakes have a cream cheese filling swirled with the batter. For Hot Fudge Brownie Sundae Cupcakes, the cupcakes are split and filled with a thick layer of ice cream. Lemon Poppy Seed Butterfly Cupcakes have a generous mound of eye-catching lemon cream holding little cupcake wings.

MOST OF THESE CUPCAKES ARE OF THE SIT-DOWN-DESSERT TYPE, AND ARE BEST SERVED ON INDIVIDUAL PLATES AND WITH FORKS.

:: chocolate mousse cupcakes ::

Chocolate mousse—very generous. Fudge topping—very thick.
Chocolate cupcake—very dark. End result—sensational.

The chocolate mousse in the middle of this cupcake is simply whipped
cream mixed with Chocolate Fudge Sauce. More of the fudge sauce is
used for the topping.

Make the cupcakes. Position a rack in the middle of the oven. Preheat the
oven to 350°F. Line 12 muffin tin cups with paper cupcake liners.

Fill each liner with a generous 1/3 cup of batter (about 6 tablespoons),
to just below the top of the liner. Bake just until the tops feel firm and a
toothpick inserted in the center comes out clean, about 20 minutes. Cool
the cupcakes for 10 minutes in the pan on a wire rack.

Use a small knife to loosen any tops that might have stuck to the top of
the pan. Carefully place the wire rack on top of the cupcakes in their pan.
Protecting your hands with pot holders and holding the pan and rack
together, invert them to release the cupcakes onto the wire rack. Turn the
cupcakes top side up to cool completely.

Frost the cupcakes. Use a sharp knife to slice the top (about a 3/8-inch-thick
slice) off each cupcake, and place the tops right side up on a wire rack.
Place the cupcake bottoms on a serving platter; set aside. Spread 1 tablespoon of the warm chocolate sauce over each top. Let sit until the sauce
is firm.

:: continued

MAKES 12 BIG-TOP CUPCAKES

CUPCAKE MAKING :
25 minutes

CUPCAKE BAKING :
350°F, for about 20 minutes

CUPCAKES

**Chocolate Sour Cream Cupcake
Batter for 18 regular cupcakes
(page 24)**

TOPPING

3/4 **cup Chocolate Fudge Sauce
(page 26), at a thick and spreadable
consistency**

:: continued

Make the filling. Put the chocolate sauce in a large bowl; set aside. In a large bowl, using an electric mixer on low speed, beat the cream, powdered sugar, and coffee granules until the coffee dissolves, about 1 minute. Beat on medium-high speed until firm peaks form. Whisk about 1 cup of the whipped cream into the chocolate sauce until no white streaks remain. Use a rubber spatula to fold in the remaining whipped cream. Using an ice cream scoop with a 1/4-cup capacity (which works best to form a smooth edge) or a large spoon, place a scoop of mousse on each cupcake bottom. Using a wide metal spatula, carefully place the cupcake tops on top of the mousse. Refrigerate to firm the chocolate topping, then cover and keep refrigerated. Serve cold.

The cupcakes can be refrigerated for up to 2 days.

FILLING

3/4 cup Chocolate Fudge Sauce (page 26), at room temperature but pourable

1 1/4 cups heavy whipping cream

2 tablespoons powdered sugar

1 teaspoon instant coffee granules

:: hot chocolate cupcakes ::

½ cup (1 stick) unsalted butter,
   cut into 6 pieces

1⅓ cups (8 ounces) semisweet chocolate
   chips or chopped semisweet
   chocolate

2   large eggs

¾   cup sugar

⅛   teaspoon salt

1   teaspoon vanilla extract

¼   cup unbleached all-purpose flour

2   tablespoons Chocolate Fudge Sauce
   (page 26), cold

Vanilla, coffee, raspberry, or
peppermint ice cream for serving

Some people fantasize about big cars or winning the lottery, but my fantasies are of the chocolate kind. Fantasy meets reality here with this warm, soft, dark chocolate fudge cupcake with a melted chocolate center that spills out when you put fork to cupcake. Making this fantasy come true was a lot easier and less expensive than buying that Porsche.

I bake these cupcakes in a muffin tin with large 1-cup-capacity cups. The cupcakes do not rise to the top of the cups, but the wide disk shape that results works well. The soft centers of the baked cupcakes sink slightly after they come out of the oven. The one teaspoon of chocolate sauce in the center may not seem like enough, but it is: if a larger amount of sauce is used, the cupcakes are so soft that they tend to fall apart when removed from the pan. (Not a complete disaster, but not too attractive.) Serve the cupcakes warm and with a scoop of ice cream—perfect.

Position a rack in the middle of the oven. Preheat the oven to 350°F. Line 6 extra-large muffin tin cups with large paper liners. Spray the paper liners with nonstick cooking spray.

Put the butter and chocolate chips in a heatproof bowl or the top of a double boiler and place it over, but not touching, a saucepan of barely simmering water (or the bottom of the double boiler). Stir until the butter and chocolate chips are melted and smooth. Remove from the water and set aside to cool slightly.

In a large bowl, using an electric mixer on medium speed, beat the eggs, sugar, salt, and vanilla until thickened and lightened in color, about 2 minutes. Stop the mixer and scrape the sides of the bowl as needed during mixing. On low speed, mix in the melted chocolate mixture. Mix in the flour until it is incorporated.

Fill each paper liner with slightly more than 1/3 cup of batter, to about 1/2 inch below the top of the liner. Put 1 teaspoon of the cold chocolate sauce in the center of each cupcake and use a small metal spatula or clean finger to spread the batter over the chocolate sauce, covering it completely.

Bake just until the tops are firm and a toothpick inserted near the edge comes out with a little sticky, but not wet, batter clinging to it, about 20 minutes. (If you test the center, you will hit the melted filling.) Cool the cupcakes for 10 to 20 minutes in the pan on a wire rack.

Carefully lift the cupcakes by their papers from the pan. Carefully remove the papers, and use a wide metal spatula to slide the cupcakes onto serving plates. Place a scoop of ice cream beside each cupcake and serve immediately.

The cupcakes can be left in their paper liners, covered, and stored at room temperature for up to 2 days. Rewarm them for about 10 minutes in a preheated 225°F oven.

:: strawberry shortcake cupcakes ::

MAKES 12 EXTRA-LARGE CUPCAKES

CUPCAKE MAKING :
20 minutes

CUPCAKE BAKING :
350°F, for about 16 minutes

CUPCAKES

2/3	cup whole milk
1	cup unbleached all-purpose flour
1	teaspoon baking powder
1/2	teaspoon salt
4	large eggs
1 1/3	cups sugar
1	teaspoon vanilla extract
1/2	teaspoon pure almond extract

My dad was a produce shipper, so I grew up with fruit coming in bushels and berries coming in flats. Mom could always count on having plenty of strawberries to serve with her light sponge-cake cupcakes that she heaped, and I mean heaped, with strawberries and loads of whipped cream. The biggest strawberries, "toppers" my dad called them, were put aside to crown each cupcake. Mmmm—it was a happy childhood.

These shortcakes are made with an old-fashioned hot milk sponge cake. Beating hot milk into the whipped eggs cooks the eggs slightly, stabilizes the fluffy batter, and consistently produces a moist, light sponge cake. Before they are filled, these cupcakes can be tightly wrapped and frozen for up to a month. Take out as many cupcakes as you need and defrost them still in their wrapping. The quantities below are for about 1/2 cup of strawberries and a generous 1/2 cup of whipped cream for each shortcake—but more is fine, too.

Make the cupcakes. Position a rack in the middle of the oven. Preheat the oven to 350°F. Line 12 extra-large muffin tin cups with large paper liners. Spray the paper liners with nonstick cooking spray.

Heat the milk in a medium saucepan over low heat just until it is hot; it should measure about 150°F on a thermometer. Remove from the heat.

Sift the flour, baking powder, and salt into a medium bowl and set aside. In a large bowl, using an electric mixer on medium speed, beat the eggs and sugar until thickened and lightened to a cream color, about 3 minutes. Stop the mixer and scrape the sides of the bowl as needed during mixing. Mix in the vanilla and almond extracts. On low speed, mix in the flour mixture until it is incorporated. Slowly add the hot milk and continue mixing for about 30 seconds, until the batter is smooth; the batter will be thin.

Fill each paper liner with a scant 1/2 cup of batter, to about 5/8 inch below the top of the liner. Bake just until the tops feel firm and a toothpick inserted in the center comes out clean, about 16 minutes. Cool the cup-cakes for 10 minutes in the pan on a wire rack.

Carefully place the wire rack on top of the cupcakes in their pan. Protecting your hands with pot holders and holding the pan and rack together, invert them to release the cupcakes onto the wire rack. Turn the cupcakes top side up to cool completely, then remove the paper liners.

Make the filling and topping. In a large bowl, stir the sliced strawberries and granulated sugar together. Let sit for 30 minutes. Some juice will be released as the strawberries sit, and they will shrink to about 6 cups.

In a large bowl, using an electric mixer on medium-high speed, beat the cream, powdered sugar, and vanilla until soft peaks form. Using a serrated knife, slice each cupcake into three layers. Place the bottom of each cup-cake on an individual serving plate. Spoon 1/4 cup of the strawberries, with their juices, onto each one, then spoon 1/4 cup whipped cream onto each. Top with the middle cupcake layers and repeat with the remaining sliced strawberries and another 1/4 cup whipped cream for each. Some sliced strawberries and whipped cream will spill onto the plates; this is good. Place the cupcake tops on top and garnish each one with a tablespoon of whipped cream and a whole strawberry. Serve immediately.

The unfilled cupcakes can be covered and stored for 1 day at room temperature.

CHOICES For a make-your-own summer party dessert, serve a platter of sliced cupcakes with big bowls of strawberries, raspberries, blueberries, or sliced peeled peaches and plenty of whipped cream and let guests create their own shortcake extravaganza. Toss blueberries or peaches with 1/3 cup sugar, as for the strawberries, but serve raspberries without sugar; stirring the raspberries with the sugar would crush them.

FILLING AND TOPPING

8   cups cleaned, stemmed, and sliced strawberries (about 5 pints), plus 12 large strawberries, cleaned and stemmed

1/3   cup granulated sugar

3   cups heavy whipping cream

1/4   cup powdered sugar

1 1/2   teaspoons vanilla extract

:: lemon poppy seed butterfly cupcakes ::

These cupcakes have wings. A slice is cut from the top of each one and a creamy filling is mounded on the cupcakes, then the slices are halved and pressed into the filling to resemble wings. In England these are called fairy cakes, a reference to the wings of a fairy. Whether it's butterflies or fairies, this lemon-filled version is just right for a spring party.

Make the cupcakes. Position a rack in the middle of the oven. Preheat the oven to 350°F. Line 12 muffin tin cups with paper cupcake liners.

Sift the flour, baking powder, baking soda, and salt into a medium bowl and set aside. In a large bowl, using an electric mixer on medium speed, beat the butter and sugar until smoothly blended and lightened in color, about 1 minute. Stop the mixer and scrape the sides of the bowl as needed during mixing. Add the eggs one at a time, beating until each is blended and the batter looks creamy, about 1 minute. Mix in the vanilla, lemon zest, and poppy seeds. On low speed, add half of the flour mixture, mixing just to incorporate it. Mix in the buttermilk to blend it. Mix in the remaining flour mixture until it is incorporated and the batter looks smooth.

Fill each paper liner with a scant 1/4 cup (about 3 1/2 tablespoons) of batter, to about 1/2 inch below the top of the liner. Bake just until the tops feel firm and a toothpick inserted in the center comes out clean, about 18 minutes. The cupcakes will rise just above the tops of the paper liners. Cool the cupcakes for 10 minutes in the pan on a wire rack.

Carefully place the wire rack on top of the cupcakes in their pan. Protecting your hands with pot holders and holding the pan and rack together, invert them to release the cupcakes onto the wire rack. Turn the cupcakes top side up to cool completely.

:: continued

MAKES 12 REGULAR CUPCAKES
::::::::::::::::::::::::
CUPCAKE MAKING :
25 minutes

CUPCAKE BAKING :
350°F, for about 18 minutes

CUPCAKES

1	cup unbleached all-purpose flour
1/2	teaspoon baking powder
1/2	teaspoon baking soda
1/4	teaspoon salt
1/4	cup (1/2 stick) unsalted butter, at room temperature
3/4	cup sugar
2	large eggs
1	teaspoon vanilla extract
2	teaspoons grated lemon zest
1	tablespoon poppy seeds
1/2	cup buttermilk (any fat content)

:: continued

:: filled cupcakes

FILLING

1   cup heavy whipping cream

2   tablespoons powdered sugar

1/2   teaspoon vanilla extract

3/4   cup plus 2 tablespoons Lemon Filling (page 27), cold

Powdered sugar for dusting

Make the filling. In a large bowl, using an electric mixer on medium-high speed, beat the cream, powdered sugar, and vanilla until firm peaks form. Using a rubber spatula, fold in 1/4 cup of the lemon filling, then swirl in 1/2 cup of the remaining sauce, leaving streaks of yellow sauce.

Use a sharp knife to slice the top (about a 1/4-inch-thick slice) off each cupcake. Dust the tops with powdered sugar, and set aside. Leaving a 1/4-inch plain edge on each cupcake bottom, use a spoon to mound about 1/4 cup filling on each. Cut the tops in half and press them into the filling, the cut sides facing out and the powdered sugar side up; tilt the halves up slightly so that they look like spread wings.

Spoon the remaining 2 tablespoons lemon filling into a small self-sealing plastic freezer bag. Press out the excess air and seal the bag. Cut off one corner of the bag to make a hole about 1/8 inch long. Hold the bag above the space between each set of wings and squeeze a thin line of lemon filling between the wings. Serve, or cover and refrigerate to serve cold.

The cupcakes can be refrigerated for up to 2 days.

chocolate-covered mint meltaway cupcakes

Meltaway candies have a chocolate mint center covered with chocolate. These cupcake meltaways duplicate the combination: there is a tender chocolate cupcake, a mint-flavored chocolate cream filling, and a fudge glaze that surrounds the cupcake. The cupcakes have their bottoms and sides covered with the glaze and are served upside down. Although this cupcake looks as if it came from a fancy bakery, it simply involves putting together three of the "Head-Start" preparations.

You will need a double recipe of the glaze for these cupcakes. They will use only about three-quarters of the double recipe, but it is easier to work with a generous quantity. Any leftover glaze can be covered and refrigerated for up to 2 weeks.

Make the cupcakes. Position a rack in the middle of the oven. Preheat the oven to 350°F. Line 12 extra-large muffin tin cups with large paper cupcake liners. Spray the inside of each liner with nonstick cooking spray.

Fill each paper liner with a generous 1/3 cup of batter, to about 1/2 inch from the top of the liner. Using a small spatula, smooth the top of the batter. Bake just until the tops feel firm and a toothpick inserted in the center comes out clean, about 20 minutes. Cool the cupcakes for 10 minutes in the pan on a wire rack.

Carefully place the wire rack on top of the cupcakes in their pan. Protecting your hands with pot holders and holding the pan and rack together, invert them to release the cupcakes onto the wire rack. Turn the cupcakes top side up to cool completely.

Make the filling. Transfer the chocolate sauce to a large bowl and stir in the peppermint extract. Cover and refrigerate until the filling is firm around the edges and the center feels cold to the touch but is still soft, about 1 1/2 hours.

:: continued

MAKES 12 EXTRA-LARGE CUPCAKES

CUPCAKE MAKING :
40 minutes

CUPCAKE BAKING :
350°F, for about 20 minutes

CUPCAKES

Chocolate Sour Cream Cupcake Batter for 12 extra-large cupcakes (page 24)

FILLING

1   recipe Chocolate Fudge Sauce (page 26), just made

1/2   teaspoon peppermint extract

TOPPING

2   recipes Chocolate Fudge Glaze (page 26), cooled to a thick but spreadable consistency

:: filled cupcakes

Remove the paper liners from the cupcakes and turn the cupcakes upside down on the wire rack. Cut the cupcakes horizontally in half and move the "tops" (which were the bottoms) to the side.

Using a whisk, beat the cold filling just until the color lightens from a dark chocolate to a medium chocolate color and it thickens slightly, about 30 seconds. Immediately use a small spatula to spread about 2 tablespoons of the filling over the bottom half of each cupcake; the filling will firm up quickly. Replace the tops.

Glaze the cupcakes. The cupcakes have a preliminary crumb coating of the glaze, then a second thick, smooth coating. Using a small spatula, spread a thin layer (about 1 1/2 tablespoons) of glaze over the sides of each cup-cake. Let the cupcakes sit for about 15 minutes for the glaze to firm.

Spread a second smooth layer of glaze, about 2 1/2 tablespoons, over the glaze on each cupcake. Let the cupcakes sit for about 30 minutes to firm the glaze. Serve the cupcakes, or use a large spatula to transfer them to a platter and refrigerate. Cover the cupcakes as soon as the glaze is firm, and serve cold.

The cupcakes can be refrigerated for up to 3 days.

CHOICES Other choices for flavoring the filling are: 2 teaspoons grated orange zest plus 1 tablespoon Grand Marnier or other orange liqueur; 2 tablespoons raspberry puree or 1 tablespoon raspberry liqueur; 1 table-spoon rum; 2 tablespoons strong coffee; or 1/2 teaspoon almond extract. Or simply leave the filling plain chocolate.

:: vanilla cheesecake crunch-top cupcakes ::

MAKES 12 EXTRA-LARGE CUPCAKES

CUPCAKE MAKING :
25 minutes

CUPCAKE BAKING :
325°F, for about 25 minutes

FILLING

1	8-ounce package cream cheese, at room temperature
1/4	cup sugar
1	large egg, at room temperature
1	teaspoon finely grated lemon zest
1	tablespoon fresh lemon juice
1/2	teaspoon vanilla extract

TOPPING

1/2	cup unbleached all-purpose flour
1/3	cup packed light brown sugar
1/8	teaspoon salt
2	tablespoons unsalted butter, melted

It's all together now—yellow cupcake batter swirled with cream cheese filling and baked with a crisp crumb topping. Three easy steps take care of filling and frosting in one fell swoop. These "sit-down" cupcakes are a good choice for a dinner party. A spoonful of fresh berries makes a nice accompaniment.

Position a rack in the middle of the oven. Preheat the oven to 325°F. Line 12 extra-large muffin tin cups with large paper cupcake liners. Spray the inside of each liner with nonstick cooking spray.

Make the filling. In a large bowl, using an electric mixer on low speed, beat the cream cheese and sugar until smoothly blended. Beat in the egg. Mix in the lemon zest, lemon juice, and vanilla. Set aside.

Make the topping. In a medium bowl, using a large spoon, stir the flour, brown sugar, and salt together. Add the melted butter and continue stirring until crumbs form.

Make the cupcakes. Spoon 3 generous tablespoons of the batter into each cupcake liner. Spoon 1 1/2 tablespoons of cream cheese filling into the center of each; the soft filling will spread slightly over the batter. Sprinkle a generous tablespoon of crumb topping over each. The paper liners will be filled to about 1/2 inch from the top.

Bake just until the edges brown lightly and a toothpick inserted in the center comes out clean, about 25 minutes. The cupcakes will rise to the top of the paper liners. Cool the cupcakes for 20 minutes in the pan on a wire rack.

Carefully place the wire rack on top of the cupcakes in their pan. Protecting your hands with pot holders and holding the pan and rack together, invert them to release the cupcakes onto the wire rack. Turn the cupcakes top side up to cool completely. If any crumbs fall off, replace them.

Dust the cooled cupcakes lightly with powdered sugar before serving.

The cupcakes can be covered and stored at room temperature for up to 2 days.

CUPCAKES

Easy-Mix Yellow Cupcake Batter for 12 regular cupcakes (page 23)

~~~~~~~~~~~~~~~~~~

Powdered sugar for dusting

:: gingerbread cupcakes with lemon filling ::

MAKES 12 REGULAR CUPCAKES

:::::::::::::::::::::::::::::

CUPCAKE MAKING :

20 minutes

CUPCAKE BAKING :

350°F, for about 20 minutes

Your first impression of these cupcakes is of dark gingerbread with a sprinkling of powdered sugar. Attractive, yes, but even better when you discover their tart lemon filling.

This spiced batter is easy to mix and can be done by hand. A trick when measuring molasses is to spray the measuring spoon with nonstick spray or rub it with oil, which prevents the molasses from sticking to the spoon.

Make the cupcakes. Position a rack in the middle of the oven. Preheat the oven to 350°F. Line 12 muffin tin cups with paper cupcake liners. Spray the inside of each liner and the top of the pan with nonstick cooking spray.

Sift the flour, baking powder, baking soda, salt, ginger, cinnamon, and cloves into a medium bowl and set aside. In a large bowl, whisk the melted butter, brown sugar, eggs, and molasses together until blended. Using a large spoon, stir in the flour mixture in 3 additions and water in 2 additions, beginning and ending with the flour mixture and stirring until the flour is incorporated and the batter looks smooth.

Fill each paper liner with 1/3 cup of batter, to about 1/4 inch below the top of the liner. Bake just until the tops feel firm and a toothpick inserted in the center comes out clean, about 20 minutes. The cupcakes will rise above the top of the paper liners. Use a small knife to cut apart any baked tops that are touching and to loosen them from the top of the pan. Cool the cupcakes for 10 minutes in the pan on a wire rack.

CUPCAKES

1 3/4 cups unbleached all-purpose flour

1   teaspoon baking powder

3/4   teaspoon baking soda

1/4   teaspoon salt

1   tablespoon ground ginger

2   teaspoons ground cinnamon

1/4   teaspoon cloves

1/4   cup (1/2 stick) unsalted butter, melted

3/4   cup packed dark brown sugar

2   large eggs

6   tablespoons molasses

3/4   cup water

3/4   cup Lemon Filling (page 27), cold
       Powdered sugar for dusting

Carefully place the wire rack on top of the cupcakes in their pan. Protecting your hands with pot holders and holding the pan and rack together, invert them to release the cupcakes onto the wire rack. Turn the cupcakes top side up to cool completely.

Fill the cupcakes. Use a small knife to slice the top off each cupcake, even with the paper liner; set the tops aside. Cut a cone-shaped piece, about 1 inch across and 1 inch deep, out of the middle of each cupcake. Discard (or eat) the little pieces of cupcake. Spoon 1 tablespoon of the lemon filling into the hole in each cupcake. Replace the cupcake tops; some of the filling may spread over the middle of the cupcakes. Serve, or cover and refrigerate to serve cold. Just before serving, dust the top of each cupcake with powdered sugar.

The cupcakes can be refrigerated for up to 2 days.

:: lemon meringue cupcakes ::

CUPCAKES

1¼ cups unbleached all-purpose flour

¾ teaspoon baking powder

¼ teaspoon salt

⅔ cup whole milk

5 tablespoons unsalted butter, cut into 5 pieces

2 large eggs

1 large egg yolk

1¼ cups sugar

1 teaspoon vanilla extract

¼ teaspoon almond extract

¾ cup Lemon Filling, (page 27), just prepared and still warm, or cold

Move over, lemon meringue pie. Hot-milk cake, another American classic, is the batter for this tender buttery cupcake with a lemon filling hiding under swirls of golden meringue. Leave the paper liners on the cupcakes when you bake the meringue so they stay moist.

Make the cupcakes. Position a rack in the middle of the oven. Preheat the oven to 350°F. Line 12 muffin tin cups with paper cupcake liners.

Sift the flour, baking powder, and salt into a medium bowl and set aside. Put the milk and butter in a small saucepan and heat over low heat just until hot; it should measure about 150°F on a thermometer. Remove from the heat.

Meanwhile, in a large bowl, using an electric mixer on medium speed, beat the eggs, egg yolk, and sugar until thickened and lightened to a cream color, about 3 minutes. Stop the mixer and scrape the sides of the bowl as needed during mixing. Add the vanilla and almond extracts. On low speed, mix in the flour mixture to incorporate it. Slowly mix in the hot milk mixture until the batter is smooth.

Fill each paper liner with a scant ⅓ cup of batter, to about ¼ inch below the top of the liner. Bake just until the tops feel firm and a toothpick inserted in the center comes out clean, about 22 minutes. Cool the cupcakes in the pan on a wire rack just until they are cool enough to handle, about 10 minutes.

Carefully place the wire rack on top of the cupcakes in their pan. Protecting your hands with pot holders and holding the pan and rack together, invert them to release the cupcakes onto the wire rack. Turn the cupcakes top side up to cool completely. (Leave the paper liners on the cupcakes so they do not dry out when baked with the meringue.)

Fill the cupcakes. Reheat the oven to 350°F. Cut a cone-shaped piece, about 1 inch across and ¾ inch deep, out of the middle of the top of each cupcake; set the pieces aside. Spoon 1 tablespoon of the lemon filling into each hole. Replace the cone-shaped pieces of cupcake. If any filling leaks out, spread it over the top of the cupcake after you replace the top.

Immediately make the meringue topping. Have a baking sheet ready. In a large bowl, beat the egg whites and cream of tartar with an electric mixer on low speed until the whites are foamy and the cream of tartar dissolves, about 1 minute. Beat on medium-high speed until soft peaks form, then beat in the sugar 1 tablespoon at a time.

Use a thin metal spatula to spread a generous ⅓ cup of meringue over the top of each cupcake, dipping the spatula gently into the meringue to make swirls. Place the cupcakes 2 inches apart on the baking sheet. Bake until the meringue is light brown, about 15 minutes.

Cool the cupcakes for 1 hour, then carefully cover and refrigerate for at least 4 hours. Remove the paper liners and serve cold.

The cupcakes can be refrigerated for up to 2 days.

MERINGUE

4   large egg whites

¼   teaspoon cream of tartar

¼   cup sugar

:: lemon coconut snowballs ::

MAKES 12 REGULAR CUPCAKES

::::::::::::::::::::::::::

CUPCAKE MAKING :

30 minutes

CUPCAKE BAKING :

350°F, for about 23 minutes

CUPCAKES

1 1/3 cups cake flour

1 teaspoon baking powder

1/8 teaspoon salt

6 tablespoons whole milk

1 teaspoon vanilla extract

1/4 teaspoon almond extract

6 tablespoons (3/4 stick) unsalted
    butter, at room temperature

1 cup sugar

6 large egg whites

1/4 teaspoon cream of tartar

3/4 cup Lemon Filling (page 27), cold

:: continued

"Snowballs, hurray!" my friends cheered when I carried these in to our New Year's Eve potluck dinner. They all had happy memories of eating these old-fashioned white cupcakes filled with lemon sauce, slathered in fluffy frosting, and covered in shredded coconut. Covering both the top and sides of these cupcakes with frosting produces the snowball effect. This white batter includes only egg whites, no yolks. Cake flour plus beaten egg whites make the texture especially light.

Make the cupcakes. Position a rack in the middle of the oven. Preheat the oven to 350°F. Line 12 muffin tin cups with paper cupcake liners.

Sift the flour, baking powder, and salt into a medium bowl and set aside. In a small bowl, stir the milk and vanilla and almond extracts together.

In a large bowl, using an electric mixer on medium speed, beat the butter and sugar until smoothly blended and lightened in color, about 2 minutes. Stop the mixer and scrape the sides of the bowl as needed during mixing. On low speed, add the flour mixture in 3 additions and the milk mixture in 2 additions, beginning and ending with the flour mixture and beating until each addition is incorporated before adding the next. Set aside.

In another large bowl, using clean beaters, beat the egg whites and cream of tartar on low speed until the whites are foamy and the cream of tartar dissolves, about 1 minute. Beat on medium-high speed until soft peaks form. Use a rubber spatula to fold one-third of the whipped egg whites into the batter, then fold in the remaining whites until no streaks of egg white remain.

Fill each paper liner with 1/3 cup of batter, to about 1/4 inch below the top of the liner. Bake just until the tops feel firm and a toothpick inserted in the center comes out clean or with a few dry crumbs clinging to it, about 23 minutes. The tops should remain pale or barely brown just on the edges. Cool the cupcakes for 10 minutes in the pan on a wire rack.

:: continued

FROSTING

3   **cups shredded sweetened coconut**

1   **recipe Seven-Minute Frosting
    (page 31)**

Carefully place the wire rack on top of the cupcakes in their pan. Protecting your hands with pot holders and holding the pan and rack together, invert them to release the cupcakes onto the wire rack. Turn the cupcakes top side up to cool completely.

Fill the cupcakes. Remove the paper liners. Cut a cone-shaped piece, about 1 inch across and 1 inch deep, out of the middle of the top of each cupcake; set the pieces aside. Spoon 1 tablespoon of lemon filling into each hole. Replace the cone-shaped pieces of cupcake. Immediately frost the cupcakes.

Frost the cupcakes. Spread the coconut on a plate or a piece of wax paper. Holding a cupcake in the palm of your hand, use a small metal spatula to spread about 1/2 cup of frosting over the top and sides, covering it completely. Sprinkle coconut generously over the frosting, letting any extra fall onto the plate to be recycled onto another cupcake. Place the cupcake on a serving plate, and continue frosting the remaining cupcakes.

Serve, or cover carefully and refrigerate to serve cold. Use a wide metal spatula to lift the cupcakes from the plate.

The cupcakes can be refrigerated for up to 2 days.

CHOICES These snowballs can also become "snowcaps." Rather than covering the top and sides of the cupcake with frosting and coconut, frost just the top of the cupcake with a generous amount of frosting, then dip the top in coconut.

:: chocolate-covered hi-hats ::

Tell someone from New York that you are making Hi-Hats, and their eyes will light up. This old-fashioned bakery specialty is a chocolate cupcake with a large mound of soft marshmallow filling hidden under a coating of chocolate. Tell someone from another part of the country that you are making Hi-Hats, and they are likely to give you a blank stare. Here is the recipe for making Hi-Hats that will make eyes light up from coast to coast.

I found that a seven-minute frosting made extra-firm with additional sugar and cooked for about 12 minutes instead of 7 was all there was to the marshmallow filling. The rest was easy—just swirl the filling on the cupcakes and coat them with chocolate.

Make the cupcakes. Position a rack in the middle of the oven. Preheat the oven to 350°F. Line 12 muffin tin cups with paper cupcake liners.

Fill each paper liner with a generous 1/3 cup of batter, to about 1/8 inch below the top of the liner. Bake just until the tops feel firm and a toothpick inserted in the center comes out clean, about 20 minutes. Cool the cupcakes for 10 minutes in the pan on a wire rack.

Use a small knife to loosen any tops that might have stuck to the top of the pan. Carefully place the wire rack on top of the cupcakes in their pan. Protecting your hands with pot holders and holding the pan and rack together, invert them to release the cupcakes onto the wire rack. Turn the cupcakes top side up to cool completely.

Make the filling. Put the sugar, water, egg whites, and cream of tartar in a heatproof container or the top of a double boiler with at least a 2-quart capacity and beat with a handheld electric mixer on high speed until opaque, white, and foamy, about 1 minute. Put the bowl over, but not touching, a saucepan of barely simmering water (or the bottom of the double boiler).

:: continued

MAKES 12 BIG-TOP CUPCAKES

CUPCAKE MAKING :
25 minutes, plus chilling time

CUPCAKE BAKING :
350°F, for about 20 minutes

CUPCAKES

Chocolate Sour Cream Cupcake Batter for 12 big-top cupcakes (page 24)

FILLING

13/4 cups sugar

1/4 cup water

3 large egg whites

1/4 teaspoon cream of tartar

1 teaspoon vanilla extract

1/2 teaspoon almond extract

COATING

2 cups (12 ounces) semisweet chocolate chips or chopped semisweet chocolate

3 tablespoons canola or vegetable oil

:: filled cupcakes

The top container should sit firmly over the pan of hot water; be sure to keep the cord of the electric mixer away from the burner. Beat on high speed until the frosting forms a stiff peak that stands straight up if you stop the beaters and lift them out of the mixture, about 12 minutes. The frosting should register 160°F on a thermometer. Remove the container from the water, add the vanilla and almond extracts, and continue beating for 2 minutes to further thicken the filling. The filling will become firmer as it cools on the finished cupcakes.

Spoon the filling into a large pastry bag fitted with a large plain pastry tip or a large plastic freezer bag with a 1/2-inch-long hole cut in one corner. Leaving a 1/8-inch plain edge on each cupcake, pipe a spiral of filling into a 2-inch-high cone-shaped mound on top of each one, using about 1/2 cup of filling per cupcake. Place the filled cupcakes on a platter and refrigerate, uncovered, while you prepare the coating.

Make the chocolate coating. Put the chocolate and oil in a heatproof bowl or the top of a double boiler and place it over, but not touching, a saucepan of barely simmering water (or the bottom of the double boiler). Stir until the chocolate is melted and smooth. Scrape the chocolate coating into a small bowl and cool slightly, about 15 minutes.

Holding each cupcake by its bottom, dip the top of the mound of filling in the chocolate coating, letting any excess drip off, then spoon more coating over the unfilled edge of the cupcake and over the rest of the filling to coat it; none of the white filling should show. (You will have some chocolate coating left for another use or to pour over ice cream, but it is easier to work with a larger quantity of chocolate coating.) Let the cupcakes sit at room temperature for about 15 minutes to firm the coating slightly.

Peel off the paper liners and discard them. (This will make for a smooth chocolate-coated edge if any coating has dripped onto the paper liner.) Return the cupcakes to the platter and refrigerate for about 30 minutes to set the coating, then cover and refrigerate for at least 2 hours. Serve cold.

The cupcakes can be refrigerated for up to 3 days.

:: hot fudge brownie sundae cupcakes ::

MAKES 12 CUPCAKE SUNDAES

::::::::::::::::::::::::::::::::

CUPCAKE MAKING :
20 minutes

CUPCAKE BAKING :
325°F, for about 30 minutes

CUPCAKES

3/4   cup (1 1/2 sticks) unsalted butter,
      cut into pieces

6   ounces unsweetened chocolate,
      chopped

3   large eggs

1 3/4 cups sugar

1/4   teaspoon salt

2   teaspoons vanilla extract

1 1/4 cups unbleached all-purpose flour

Cupcake sundaes are equally at home in a pool of chocolate sauce on your best china or eaten out of hand and dipped in the sauce for a midnight splurge. Whenever you serve them, they are handy to have ready in the freezer. Since mixing this brownie-type batter is a blending rather than a beating of ingredients, it can be mixed with a whisk.

Make the cupcakes. Position a rack in the middle of the oven. Preheat the oven to 325°F. Line 12 muffin tin cups with paper cupcake liners. Spray the paper liners with nonstick spray.

Put the butter and chocolate in a heatproof bowl or the top of a double boiler and place it over, but not touching, a saucepan of barely simmering water (or the bottom of the double boiler). Stir until the butter and chocolate are melted and smooth. Remove from the water and set aside to cool slightly.

In a large bowl, whisk the eggs, sugar, and salt to blend them thoroughly, about 1 minute. Whisk in the slightly cooled chocolate mixture and vanilla to incorporate them. Whisk in the flour just until no white streaks remain.

Fill each paper liner with about 1/3 cup of batter, to about 1/4 inch below the top of the liner.

Bake just until the tops feel firm and a toothpick inserted in the center comes out with a few moist crumbs clinging to it, about 30 minutes. The cupcakes will rise about 1/2 inch above the top of the paper liners. Cool the cupcakes for 10 minutes in the pan on a wire rack.

Carefully place the wire rack on top of the cupcakes in their pan. Protecting your hands with pot holders and holding the pan and rack together, invert them to release the cupcakes onto the wire rack. Turn the cupcakes top side up to cool completely.

Fill the cupcakes. Remove the paper liners from the filled cupcakes. Cut the cupcakes horizontally in half. Place 1/4 cup of the ice cream on the bottom half of a cupcake; an ice cream scoop with 1/4-cup capacity works well and makes a smoothly rounded ball of ice cream. Replace the top; do not press down on the ice cream, but leave it as a thick 1-inch layer. Wrap the cupcake in plastic wrap. Continue to fill and wrap the remaining cupcakes, then seal them in a container. Freeze for at least 5 hours.

Unwrap the ice cream cupcakes and serve with the warm chocolate sauce spooned around them.

The cupcakes can be frozen for up to 1 week.

2 pints ice cream (vanilla, peppermint, coffee, or chocolate chip make good choices), softened just until spreadable

1 recipe Chocolate Fudge Sauce (page 26), warmed

:: boston cream pie cupcakes ::

MAKES 12 EXTRA-LARGE CUPCAKES
: :

CUPCAKE MAKING :
25 minutes

CUPCAKE BAKING :
350°F, for about 16 minutes

FILLING

1½ cups whole milk

½ cup sugar

4 large egg yolks

3 tablespoons unbleached all-purpose flour

1 teaspoon vanilla extract

CUPCAKES

⅔ cup whole milk

1 cup unbleached all-purpose flour

1 teaspoon baking powder

½ teaspoon salt

4 large eggs

1⅓ cups sugar

2 teaspoons vanilla extract

Boston Cream Pie is not a pie at all, but a yellow cake filled with vanilla pastry cream (a.k.a. vanilla pudding) and frosted with chocolate glaze. It seems quite natural, then, to take this pie that is a cake and turn it into a cupcake.

To prevent spoilage, vanilla pastry cream should be kept refrigerated at all times, for no longer than 3 days.

Make the filling. In a medium saucepan, heat the milk over low heat, just until it is hot; it should measure about 150°F on a thermometer. Remove from the heat.

Meanwhile, in a medium bowl, whisk the sugar and egg yolks until smooth. Whisk in the flour until smooth. Whisking constantly, slowly pour the hot milk into the yolk mixture, then pour it back into the saucepan. Cook over medium heat, stirring constantly with a wooden spoon, until it thickens and just comes to a boil; stir often where the bottom and sides of the pan meet to prevent scorching. Reduce the heat to low and cook at a gentle boil for 1 minute, stirring constantly. Remove the pan from the heat and pour the pastry cream through a fine strainer into a medium bowl. (Discard any bits in the strainer.) Stir in the vanilla. Press a piece of plastic wrap onto the surface of the pastry cream and use the tip of a knife to poke a few holes in the plastic wrap to let steam escape. Refrigerate for 2 hours, or until cool to the touch and thickened further.

Make the cupcakes. Position a rack in the middle of the oven. Preheat the oven to 350°F. Line 12 extra-large muffin tin cups with large paper cupcake liners. Spray the paper liners with nonstick cooking spray.

In a medium saucepan, heat the milk over low heat just until it is hot; it should measure about 150°F on a thermometer. Remove from the heat.

Sift the flour, baking powder, and salt into a medium bowl and set aside. In a large bowl, using an electric mixer on medium speed, beat the eggs and sugar until thickened and lightened to a cream color, about 3 minutes. Stop the mixer and scrape the sides of the bowl as needed during mixing. Mix in the vanilla. On low speed, mix in the flour mixture until it is incorporated. Slowly add the hot milk and continue mixing for about 30 seconds, until the batter is smooth; the batter will be thin.

Fill each paper liner with a scant 1/2 cup of batter, to about 5/8 inch below the top of the liner. Bake just until the tops feel firm and a toothpick inserted in the center comes out clean, about 16 minutes. Cool the cupcakes for 10 minutes in the pan on a wire rack.

Carefully place the wire rack on top of the cupcakes in their pan. Protecting your hands with pot holders and holding the pan and rack together, invert them to release the cupcakes onto the wire rack. Turn the cupcakes top side up to cool completely.

Fill the cupcakes. Remove the paper liners from the cupcakes. Use a serrated knife to slice the top (about a 1/4-inch-thick slice) off each cupcake; set the tops aside. Cut a cone-shaped piece, about 1 inch across and 1 inch deep, out of the middle of each cupcake. Discard (or eat) the little pieces. Spoon about 1 1/2 tablespoons of the cold pastry cream into the hole in each cupcake. Replace the cupcake tops; some of the filling may spread over the middle of the cupcakes when the tops are replaced.

Frost the cupcakes. Using a thin metal spatula, spread 1 tablespoon of the chocolate glaze over each cupcake top, and replace them on top of the cupcakes. Serve, or cover and refrigerate to serve cold.

The cupcakes can be refrigerated for up to 2 days.

TOPPING

3/4 cup Chocolate Glaze (page 26), at a thick and spreadable consistency

chapter 5:

CELEBRATION CUPCAKES

• • •

• • •

Although I think that all cupcakes are ready to party, this group is geared to specific **CELEBRATIONS,** ready to cheer or to cheer up. There are cupcakes for tea parties, for times that call for something indulgent and gorgeous, for celebrating the bounty of the season, and for festive holidays.

• • •

MANY OF THESE CUPCAKES HAVE SPECIAL FINISHES. SWIRLS OF FROSTING COVER HUMMINGBIRD CUPCAKES WHILE FUDGE BALL CUPCAKES LOOK LIKE FANCY CANDIES. OTHER CUPCAKES ARE TOPPED WITH SIMPLE-TO-MAKE CANDY FLOWERS. HALLOWEEN CUPCAKES HAVE A SPIDERWEB DECORATION, FRESH CRAN-BERRIES DECORATE THANKSGIVING TEA CAKES, AND VALENTINE'S DAY CUPCAKES HAVE HEART-STEALING CHOCOLATE HEARTS. FOR CHRISTMAS, THERE ARE BOTH AN ELEGANT WINTER WHITE CUPCAKE AND AN INFORMAL HOLIDAY CUPCAKE DECORATED WITH PEPPERMINT CANDY. AND THERE ARE CUPCAKES BAKED IN ICE CREAM CONES. CALL YOUR FRIENDS, INVITE THE FAMILY, GET THE KIDS, AND CELEBRATE WITH THESE CUPCAKES ALL YEAR LONG.

:: chocolate-covered brownie ice cream cone cupcakes ::

If ever a cupcake was made for pure fun, it is this one. Kids and grown-ups alike will get a kick out of eating a fudge brownie cupcake covered in chocolate coating and sprinkles from an ice cream cone.

Surprisingly, the ice cream cones do not change color when they bake; they just become more pleasantly crisp. Use ice cream cones with flat bottoms, which will stand straight up in the pan. Put a square of foil in the bottom of each muffin cup and wrap it around the cone to hold it in place. Ice cream cones come in several sizes; those in packages that weigh 1.76 ounces and have 12 cones are the best size to use. If filled with about ¼ cup of batter, the cupcakes will rise to form nicely rounded, bumpy tops that look like a generous scoop of ice cream.

Make the cupcakes. Position a rack in the middle of the oven. Preheat the oven to 325°F. Cut twelve 6-inch squares of aluminum foil and press them into 12 regular or mini-muffin tin cups, letting the edges of the foil over-hang the edges. Place a cone in each cup, wrapping the foil around the cone to hold it sturdily in the muffin cup. If you jiggle the pan slightly, the cones should not fall over.

Put the butter and unsweetened chocolate in a heatproof bowl or the top of a double boiler and place it over, but not touching, a saucepan of barely simmering water (or the bottom of the double boiler). Stir until the butter and chocolate are melted and smooth. Remove from the water and set aside to cool slightly.

In a small bowl, stir the flour, baking powder, and salt together; set aside. In a large bowl, using an electric mixer on medium speed, beat the eggs and sugar until thickened and lightened in color, about 1 minute. Stop the mixer and scrape the sides of the bowl as needed during mixing. Mix in the vanilla. On low speed, mix in the chocolate mixture. Mix in the flour mixture until it is incorporated and the batter looks smooth. Mix in the chocolate chips.

:: continued

MAKES 12
ICE CREAM CONE CUPCAKES

:::::::::::::::::::::::

CUPCAKE MAKING :
20 minutes

CUPCAKE BAKING :
325°F, for about 28 minutes

CUPCAKES

- **12**   flat-bottomed ice cream cones
- **½**   cup (1 stick) unsalted butter, cut into pieces
- **3**   ounces unsweetened chocolate, chopped
- **¾**   cup unbleached all-purpose flour
- **½**   teaspoon baking powder
- **¼**   teaspoon salt
- **2**   large eggs
- **1¼**   cups sugar
- **1**   teaspoon vanilla extract
- **⅔**   cup (4 ounces) semisweet chocolate chips

:: continued

:: celebration cupcakes

Using a small spoon, fill each ice cream cone with about ¼ cup batter, to just below the top of the cone. Carefully put the cupcakes in the oven, making sure that the cones are still standing upright. Bake just until a toothpick inserted in the center comes out with moist crumbs, but not wet batter, clinging to it, about 28 minutes. (If the toothpick penetrates chocolate chips, test another spot.) Let the cupcakes cool in the pan for about 20 minutes.

Meanwhile, make the chocolate coating. Put the chocolate and oil in a heat-proof bowl or the top of a double boiler and place it over, but not touching, a saucepan of barely simmering water (or the bottom of the double boiler). Stir until the chocolate is melted and smooth. Scrape the chocolate coating into a small bowl.

Dip the top of each cupcake cone in the chocolate coating, letting any excess drip off, and replace the cones in the muffin tin. (You will have some chocolate coating left over for another use or to pour over ice cream; working with a larger quantity of chocolate coating makes for easier dipping.) Let the coating firm for about 10 minutes, then sprinkle it lightly with sprinkles.

Let the cupcakes sit until the coating is firm, about 2 hours, or less if the kitchen is cool. Or, to speed the firming of the chocolate, carefully refrigerate the cupcakes in the pan for about 15 minutes; serve at room temperature. The cupcake cones can be eaten out of hand or set in small glasses or serving dishes and served as "sit-down" cupcakes.

The cupcakes can be covered and stored at room temperature for up to 3 days.

CHOICES For a festive presentation, wrap a colorful napkin around each cone before serving it.

COATING

1⅓ cups (8 ounces) semisweet chocolate chips or chopped semisweet chocolate

2 tablespoons canola or vegetable oil

1 tablespoon colored sprinkles, nonpareils, or other small sugar decorations

:: Raspberry Ice Cream Cone Cupcakes (pictured left), page 120 ::

:: butter almond tea cakes ::

CUPCAKES

1 1/4 cups unbleached all-purpose flour

1/2 teaspoon baking powder

1/2 teaspoon baking soda

1/4 teaspoon salt

1/2 cup (1 stick) unsalted butter, at room temperature

3/4 cup plus 1 tablespoon sugar

1/2 cup (3 1/2 ounces) almond paste, at room temperature

2 large eggs

1/2 teaspoon vanilla extract

1/2 teaspoon almond extract

1/2 cup buttermilk (any fat content)

"Tea cakes" are small cupcakes that bake in mini-muffin tins. Typically, tea cakes have a glaze or powdered sugar topping rather than a frosting that could drop onto pretty party clothes. These butter almond cakes are made from a light pound cake–type batter that is enriched with almond paste. The powdered sugar glaze for the top can be spread either on the warm cupcakes, so it melts slightly and becomes translucent, or on the cooled cupcakes, to produce a more opaque topping.

Almond paste is a finely ground mixture of almonds and sugar that can be found in the baking section of most supermarkets. When fresh, it is soft and malleable and combines smoothly with other ingredients. Make sure you buy almond paste rather than marzipan, which has more sugar. Most almond paste comes in 7-ounce packages, so the amount for this recipe is half of a package. The King Arthur Flour Baker's Catalogue (see Mail-Order Sources, page 141) sells almond paste in 1-pound cans.

Make the cupcakes. Position a rack in the middle of the oven. Preheat the oven to 325°F. Line 4 mini-muffin tins that have 12 cups each with mini–paper liners. Spray the paper liners with nonstick spray.

Sift the flour, baking powder, baking soda, and salt into a medium bowl and set aside. In a large bowl, using an electric mixer on medium speed, beat the butter, sugar, and almond paste until smoothly blended, about 1 minute. Stop the mixer and scrape the sides of the bowl as needed during mixing. Add the eggs one at a time, mixing until each is blended into the batter. Add the vanilla and almond extracts and beat for 2 minutes, or until the batter is smooth. On low speed, add the flour mixture in 3 additions and the buttermilk in 2 additions, beginning and ending with the flour mixture and mixing just until the flour is incorporated and the batter looks smooth.

Fill each paper liner with a slightly rounded tablespoon of batter, to about ¼ inch below the top of the liner. Bake just until the tops feel firm and a toothpick inserted in the center comes out clean, about 18 minutes. Cool the cupcakes for 5 minutes in the pan on a wire rack.

Carefully place a wire rack on top of one pan of cupcakes. Protecting your hands with pot holders and holding the pan and rack together, invert them to release the cupcakes onto the wire rack. Turn the cupcakes top side up to cool. Repeat with the remaining cupcakes. Glaze the cupcakes while they are warm or after they cool: the different results are described below.

Make the glaze. In a small bowl, whisk the powdered sugar, melted butter, 1½ tablespoons milk, and almond extract until a smooth, syrupy glaze forms. Add up to 1 tablespoon more milk by the teaspoon if needed to achieve the proper consistency.

Use a small spatula to spread a thin layer of glaze over the top of each cupcake, using about ½ teaspoon for each: if spread on warm cupcakes, the glaze will melt and become shiny, and the cupcake tops will show through it; if spread on cooled cupcakes, the glaze will be white and opaque. The glaze will become firm as it sets. Arrange 3 or more sliced almonds over the soft frosting on top of each cupcake, if desired.

The cupcakes can be covered and stored at room temperature for up to 2 days.

CHOICES If you have only 2 pans, halve all of the ingredients and make 24 teacakes.

GLAZE

1 cup powdered sugar

2 tablespoons unsalted butter, melted

1½ to 2½ tablespoons whole milk

¼ teaspoon almond extract

~~~~~~~~~~~~~~~~~~~~~~~~~

½ cup toasted (see page 16) sliced almonds (optional)

:: lemon sponge tea cakes ::

CUPCAKES

3/4 cup unbleached all-purpose flour

1/8 teaspoon salt

4 large eggs, separated

1¼ cups sugar

2 teaspoons finely grated lemon zest

2 tablespoons fresh lemon juice

GLAZE (optional)

1/2 cup powdered sugar

1 tablespoon unsalted butter, melted

1 tablespoon plus 1 teaspoon fresh
   lemon juice

Powdered sugar for dusting
(optional)

Here is the complete original version of this recipe: "Weight of the eggs in sugar. Half of the weight of eggs in flour. Juice and rind of 2 lemons." Happily, my friend Susan Snead translated this heirloom recipe from her Grandmother Nolting to a more familiar recipe style. There is no leavening in these tea cakes: they depend on thoroughly beaten egg yolks and well-beaten whites for their featherlight texture.

To produce the desired lightly browned sides, these cupcakes are not baked in paper liners. Use nonstick pans if you have them so the cupcakes will release easily. Susan either glazes the cupcakes with lemon glaze or simply dusts them with powdered sugar.

Make the cupcakes. Position a rack in the middle of the oven. Preheat the oven to 350°F. Have ready 4 mini-muffin tins with 12 cups each, preferably nonstick. Spray the inside of each cup with nonstick cooking spray.

Sift the flour and salt into a small bowl and set aside. In a large bowl, using an electric mixer on medium speed, beat the egg yolks and sugar until thickened and lightened to a cream color, about 2 minutes. Stop the mixer and scrape the sides of the bowl as needed during mixing. On low speed, mix in the lemon zest and lemon juice. Set aside.

In another large bowl, with clean beaters, beat the egg whites on medium-high speed until they look shiny and smooth and the beaters form lines in the whites. If you stop the mixer and lift up the beaters, the whites should cling to the beaters. Using a rubber spatula, stir about one-third of the beaten egg whites into the reserved yolk mixture. Fold in the remaining egg whites just until no white streaks remain. The batter will be quite liquid but fluffy.

Using a small spoon, fill each mini-muffin cup with a generous tablespoon of batter, to about 1/4 inch below the top of the pan. Bake just until the tops feel firm and a toothpick inserted in the center comes out dry, about 10 minutes. Cool the cupcakes for 10 minutes in the pans on wire racks.

Using a small knife, loosen the sides of each cupcake from each pan. Invert the pan to release the cupcakes onto the wire racks to cool completely. If any cupcakes stick to the pan, use your fingers and the knife to gently ease them from the pan.

If making the glaze. In a small bowl, whisk the powdered sugar, melted butter, and lemon juice until smooth and syrupy. Using a small spatula, spread a thin layer of glaze over the top of each cupcake, about 1/4 teaspoon for each. Or, dust the cupcakes with powdered sugar, if desired.

The cupcakes can be covered and stored at room temperature for up to 2 days.

CHOICES Lime juice and zest can be substituted for the lemon.

If you have only 2 pans, halve all the ingredients and make 24 teacakes.

:: fudge ball cupcakes ::

MAKES 24 MINI-CUPCAKES

:::::::::::::::::::::::::::::

CUPCAKE MAKING :

30 minutes, plus standing time for coating

CUPCAKE BAKING :

325°F, for about 24 minutes

CUPCAKES

1/2	cup (1 stick) unsalted butter, cut into pieces
4	ounces unsweetened chocolate, chopped
2	large eggs
1 1/4	cups sugar
1/4	teaspoon salt
1	teaspoon vanilla extract
3/4	cup unbleached all-purpose flour

These mini–fudge brownie cupcakes coated with chocolate resemble candy truffles, but instead of candy inside the coating, you will find an extremely dark, fudgy brownie. Dusting the tops with cocoa powder or sprinkling them with colored or chocolate sprinkles, chopped nuts, or toasted coconut adds a professional candy-store finish. Arranged in a holiday tin, these cupcakes make a sweet gift.

Make the cupcakes. Position a rack in the middle of the oven. Preheat the oven to 325°F. Line 2 mini-muffin tins that have 12 cups each with mini–paper liners. Spray the paper liners with nonstick spray.

Put the butter and unsweetened chocolate in a heatproof bowl or the top of a double boiler and place it over, but not touching, a saucepan of barely simmering water (or the bottom of the double boiler). Stir the butter and chocolate until melted and smooth. Remove from the water and set aside to cool slightly.

In a large bowl, whisk the eggs, sugar, and salt to blend them thoroughly, about 1 minute. Whisk in the slightly cooled chocolate mixture and vanilla to incorporate them. Whisk in the flour just until no white streaks remain.

Fill each paper liner with about 1 1/2 tablespoons batter, to just below the top of the liner. Bake just until the tops feel firm and a toothpick inserted in the center comes out with a few moist crumbs clinging to it, about 24 minutes. Cool the cupcakes for 10 minutes in the pans on wire racks.

Using a small knife, loosen any cupcake tops that might have stuck to the pans. Carefully place a wire rack on top of one pan of cupcakes. Protecting your hands with pot holders and holding the pan and rack together, invert them to release the cupcakes onto the wire rack. Turn the cupcakes top side up to cool completely. If any cupcake tops should separate from the cupcakes when you unmold them, simply press them back on; they will stick to these moist cupcakes. Repeat with the second pan of cupcakes.

Make the chocolate coating. Put the chocolate and oil in a heatproof bowl or the top of a double boiler and place it over, but not touching, a saucepan of barely simmering water (or the bottom of the double boiler). Stir until the chocolate is melted and smooth. Scrape the chocolate coating into a small bowl.

Remove the paper liners from the cooled cupcakes. Holding the top of a cupcake with your fingers, dip all of the cupcake except the top in the chocolate coating. Gently roll it in the chocolate to coat it thoroughly, then hold it over the bowl to let any excess drip off and return the cupcake to the wire rack, uncoated top down. Repeat with the remaining cupcakes; do not let the coated cupcakes touch one another. Let sit until the chocolate coating becomes just sticky to the touch but is no longer liquid.

Use a strainer to dust the tops of the cupcakes lightly with cocoa powder. (If the chocolate is at the semifirm, sticky stage, the cocoa powder will remain on the surface, not dissolve into it.) Let the cupcakes sit at room temperature until the coating is firm, about 1½ hours. Or, to speed the firming of the chocolate, refrigerate the fudge balls on the wire racks for about 10 minutes.

When the chocolate is completely firm, put the fudge balls in clean paper liners. Cover and refrigerate. Serve cold or at room temperature.

The cupcakes can be refrigerated for up to 5 days.

CHOICES Instead of cocoa, sprinkle 1 cup toasted coconut, ½ cup chocolate sprinkles, or ¾ cup finely chopped pecans or walnuts over the chocolate-covered fudge balls. To toast coconut, spread shredded, sweetened coconut on a baking sheet and bake in a preheated 325°F oven until golden, about 11 minutes, stirring the coconut twice to help it toast evenly.

COATING

2   cups (12 ounces) semisweet chocolate chips or chopped semisweet chocolate

3   tablespoons canola or vegetable oil

Cocoa powder for dusting

:: ice cream bonbon cupcakes ::

MAKES 12 MINI-CUPCAKES

CUPCAKE MAKING :

15 minutes, plus chilling time

CUPCAKE BAKING :

none

4 ounces semisweet or bittersweet chocolate, chopped

1 pint ice cream of your choice, softened just until spreadable

Two ingredients—chocolate and ice cream—are all you need for these bite-size cupcakes. Paper cupcake liners act as molds for the chocolate cups, which are then filled with ice cream. Think of these when you want to cool off on a hot summer day, serve a lighthearted dessert at a spring party, or liven up a frosty night—in other words, just about anytime.

The ingredients can be doubled or tripled to make more cupcakes; if serving these for dessert, count on at least 3 per person. For "painting" the chocolate onto the paper liners, use a pastry brush that is narrow enough (1/2 to 1 inch) to fit easily into the liners. The paper liners are easily removed from the chocolate cups after they are filled with ice cream, but if you try to remove the paper before filling them, the cups may shatter. It's fun to fill the cups with a colorful assortment of ice cream flavors.

Make the cupcakes. Line a mini-muffin tin that has 12 cups with mini–paper liners. Use 2 liners in each: double papers are more stable to hold onto as they are coated.

Put the chocolate in a heatproof bowl or the top of a double boiler and place it over, but not touching, a saucepan of barely simmering water (or the bottom of the double boiler). Stir until the chocolate is melted and smooth. Remove from the water.

Put 1 1/2 teaspoons of the melted chocolate in a paper liner and, using a pastry brush no wider than 1 inch, brush the chocolate up the sides of the paper liner, coating it completely: be careful not to coat the top edge of the paper liners, which would make it difficult to peel the liner from the chocolate. Make sure the sides are coated evenly. Coat the remaining liners. Put the chocolate cups on a baking sheet and freeze them for at least 1 hour, or overnight.

Using a small spoon, fill each chocolate cup with about 2 tablespoons of ice cream, pressing it gently into the cup and mounding it above the top. Return the cupcakes to the baking sheet and then the freezer to firm.

Once the ice cream is firm, peel the paper liners from the chocolate and place each cupcake in a clean paper liner. Serve, or wrap individually in plastic wrap and return to the freezer.

The wrapped cupcakes can be frozen for up to 1 week.

:: fruity, nutty harvest cupcakes ::

Pecans, walnuts, almonds, apricots, dates, and cranberries make these cupcakes a celebration of the fall harvest that can carry you right through winter. With the brown sugar batter loaded with 3 cups of fruit and nuts, and even more of them garnishing the butter rum frosting, there is probably more fruit and nuts in these cupcakes than cake.

This is a long ingredient list, but they are all easily found supermarket items and many may already be (or are very nice to have) on hand. These cupcakes are good "keepers," so making a double recipe is not a bad idea. New crops of nuts appear in the supermarket beginning in October and throughout the fall. This is a good time to stock up on a year's supply to store in the freezer. Be sure to defrost the nuts before using them in the recipe, or they will chill the batter and affect the baking time.

Make the cupcakes. Position a rack in the middle of the oven. Preheat the oven to 325°F. Line 12 muffin tin cups with paper cupcake liners. Spray the inside of each liner with nonstick cooking spray.

Sift the flour, baking powder, salt, and cinnamon into a medium bowl and set aside. In a large bowl, using an electric mixer on medium speed, beat the butter, brown sugar, and granulated sugar until smoothly blended and lightened in color, about 2 minutes. Stop the mixer and scrape the sides of the bowl as needed during mixing. Beat in the eggs one at a time, beating well after each addition. Mix in the rum and vanilla. On low speed, mix in the flour mixture just until it is incorporated. Stir in the pecans, walnuts, almonds, apricots, cranberries, and dates. The batter will be thick.

Fill each paper liner with a generous 1/3 cup of batter, to about 1/8 inch below the top of the liner. Bake just until the tops feel firm and a toothpick inserted in the center comes out clean, about 35 minutes. Cool the cupcakes for 10 minutes in the pan on a wire rack.

:: continued

MAKES 12 REGULAR CUPCAKES

CUPCAKE MAKING :
20 minutes

CUPCAKE BAKING :
325°F, for about 35 minutes

CUPCAKES

1 1/3 cups unbleached all-purpose flour

1/2 teaspoon baking powder

1/4 teaspoon salt

1 teaspoon ground cinnamon

1/2 cup (1 stick) unsalted butter, melted and cooled slightly

2/3 cup packed light brown sugar

1/3 cup granulated sugar

2 large eggs

1 tablespoon rum, preferably dark

1 teaspoon vanilla extract

1/2 cup (about 2 ounces) finely chopped pecans

1/2 cup (about 2 ounces) finely chopped walnuts

:: continued

Carefully place the wire rack on top of the cupcakes in their pan. Protecting your hands with pot holders and holding the pan and rack together, invert them to release the cupcakes onto the wire rack. Turn the cupcakes top side up to cool completely.

Make the frosting. In a large bowl, using an electric mixer on low speed, beat the butter and powdered sugar until blended but still crumbly. Add the rum and vanilla and beat until smooth and creamy, about 2 minutes. The frosting will be thick.

Use a small metal spatula to spread about 1 1/2 tablespoons of frosting over the top of each cupcake, then spoon about 1 1/2 teaspoons of the mixed fruit and nuts over the top.

The cupcakes can be covered and stored at room temperature for up to 4 days.

CHOICES Other dried fruits or just one or two kinds of fruits or nuts can be used, keeping the total quantity at 3 cups. Other fruit choices include dark or golden raisins, dried pineapple, currants, dried cherries, and dried pears. Mix and match them in flavors that appeal to you.

These cupcakes freeze well, and that is an especially good idea if making a double recipe; add the fruit topping after they defrost. Freeze the cupcakes unwrapped to firm the frosting, then wrap each in plastic wrap, pack them in one layer in a plastic container, and seal it. Defrost the cupcakes in the refrigerator in the container.

The frosting can be omitted and the cupcakes finished with a dusting of powdered sugar.

1/4 cup (about 1 ounce) coarsely chopped unblanched almonds

3/4 cup (about 4 1/2 ounces) dried apricots, cut into small pieces

1/2 cup (about 2 ounces) dried cranberries

1/2 cup (about 3 ounces) chopped dates

FROSTING

6 tablespoons (3/4 stick) unsalted butter, at room temperature

1 1/2 cups powdered sugar

1 tablespoon rum, preferably dark

1/2 teaspoon vanilla extract

1/3 cup mixed chopped nuts, dried apricots, and dried cranberries for topping

:: raspberry ice cream cone cupcakes ::

MAKES 12
ICE CREAM CONE CUPCAKES

:::::::::::::::::::::::::

CUPCAKE MAKING :
20 minutes

CUPCAKE BAKING :
350°F. for about 30 minutes

CUPCAKES

12	flat-bottomed ice cream cones
1	cup unbleached all-purpose flour
1	teaspoon baking powder
1/8	teaspoon salt
1/2	cup whole milk
1	teaspoon vanilla extract
1/4	teaspoon almond extract
6	tablespoons (3/4 stick) unsalted butter, at room temperature
1	cup sugar
5	large egg whites
1/4	teaspoon cream of tartar
1	cup fresh raspberries or defrosted frozen unsweetened raspberries

Once I saw the spectacular results of my Chocolate-Covered Brownie Ice Cream Cone Cupcakes, I had to rein myself in from making dozens of cupcakes in ice cream cones. I narrowed down my choices to one more, settling on this party-in-a-cone pink raspberry version. The cones hold raspberries baked in a white cupcake batter and have a raspberry cream cheese frosting. Multicolored sprinkles or tiny candy hearts look just right for the decoration. The King Arthur Flour Baker's Catalogue (see Mail-Order Sources, page 141) sells the perfect mixture of pink, white, and red sprinkles mixed with tiny sugar hearts.

Make the cupcakes. Position a rack in the middle of the oven. Preheat the oven to 350°F. Cut twelve 6-inch squares of aluminum foil and press them into 12 regular or mini-muffin tin cups, letting the edges of the foil overhang the edges. Place a cone in each cup, wrapping the foil around the cone to hold it sturdily in the muffin cup. If you jiggle the pan slightly, the cones should not fall over.

Sift the flour, baking powder, and salt into a medium bowl and set aside.

In a small bowl, stir the milk and vanilla and almond extracts together; set aside.

In a large bowl, using an electric mixer on medium speed, beat the butter and sugar until smoothly blended and lightened in color, about 2 minutes. Stop the mixer and scrape the sides of the bowl as needed during mixing. On low speed, add the flour mixture in 3 additions and the milk mixture in 2 additions, beginning and ending with the flour mixture and beating until each addition is incorporated before adding the next. Set aside.

In another large bowl, using clean beaters, beat the egg whites with the cream of tartar on low speed until the whites are foamy and the cream of tartar dissolves, about 1 minute. Beat on medium-high speed until soft peaks form. Use a rubber spatula to fold one-third of the whipped egg whites into the reserved batter, then fold in the remaining whites until no streaks of egg white remain. Gently fold in the raspberries.

Using a small spoon, fill each ice cream cone with about ¼ cup batter, to just below the top of the cone. Carefully put the cupcakes in the oven, making sure that the cones are still standing upright. Bake until the cupcake tops are golden and a toothpick inserted in the center comes out dry, about 30 minutes. Let the cupcakes cool in the pan for about 20 minutes.

Meanwhile, make the frosting. Process the raspberries in a food processor until smooth. Strain the puree through a fine strainer into a small bowl; discard any seeds and pulp left in the strainer. You will have about ⅓ cup of puree. Set aside.

In a large bowl, using an electric mixer on low speed, beat the butter, cream cheese, and almond extract until smooth and thoroughly blended, about 1 minute. Gradually, add the powdered sugar, mixing until smooth, about 1 minute. Mix in the raspberry puree, then beat on medium speed for 1 minute to lighten the frosting.

Use a small metal spatula to spread about 2½ tablespoons of frosting thickly over the top of each cupcake. Sprinkle the frosting lightly with sprinkles. The cupcake cones can be eaten out of hand or propped individually in small glasses or serving dishes and served as "sit-down" cupcakes.

The cupcakes can be covered and stored in the refrigerator for up to 3 days. Let sit at room temperature for 20 minutes before serving.

CHOICES For a festive presentation, wrap a colorful napkin around each cone before serving it

FROSTING

- **1** cup fresh raspberries or defrosted frozen unsweetened raspberries
- **6** tablespoons (¾ stick) unsalted butter, at room temperature
- **4** ounces cream cheese, at room temperature
- **½** teaspoon almond extract
- **2½** cups powdered sugar

- **1** tablespoon colored sprinkles, nonpareils, or other small sugar decorations, preferably pastel colors

:: spiderweb pumpkin ginger cupcakes ::

The cream cheese frosting on these deep golden orange cupcakes is decorated with a spiderweb design that is surprisingly easy to make. They are perfect for Halloween, of course, but really fit in throughout the "chilly" season. Chopped crystallized ginger adds a hot, spicy kick to the cupcakes, and it could also be used on top of the frosting as an alternative to the spiderweb decoration.

Make the cupcakes. Position a rack in the middle of the oven. Preheat the oven to 325°F. Line 12 muffin tin cups with paper cupcake liners.

Sift the flour, baking powder, baking soda, salt, cinnamon, and ginger into a medium bowl and set aside. In a large bowl, using an electric mixer on low-medium speed, beat the melted butter, sugar, and pumpkin until smoothly blended. Mix in the eggs and crystallized ginger. On low speed, mix in the flour mixture until it is incorporated. The batter will be thick.

Fill each paper liner with a generous 1/4 cup of batter, to about 1/2 inch below the top of the liner. Bake just until the tops feel firm and a toothpick inserted in the center comes out clean, about 25 minutes. Cool the cupcakes for 10 minutes in the pan on a wire rack.

Carefully place the wire rack on top of the cupcakes in their pan. Protecting your hands with pot holders and holding the pan and rack together, invert them to release the cupcakes onto the wire rack. Turn the cupcakes top side up to cool completely.

:: continued

CUPCAKES

1 1/2 cups unbleached all-purpose flour

3/4 teaspoon baking powder

3/4 teaspoon baking soda

1/4 teaspoon salt

1 teaspoon ground cinnamon

1 teaspoon ground ginger

1/2 cup (1 stick) unsalted butter, melted and cooled slightly

1 cup sugar

1 cup canned pumpkin (not pumpkin pie filling)

3 large eggs

1/4 cup (about 1 1/4 ounces) crystallized ginger cut into 1/8- to 1/4-inch pieces

:: continued

FROSTING

1   recipe Cream Cheese Frosting
    (page 25), at room temperature

1/2   to 1 teaspoon ground cinnamon

1   to 2 teaspoons whole milk

Frost the cupcakes. Transfer 1/4 cup of the frosting to a small bowl, and stir in enough cinnamon to make the frosting a light brown color and enough milk to make a thick but pourable frosting. Set aside to use for the spider-web decoration. Use a small spatula to spread a scant 1/4 cup of the remaining frosting on top of each cupcake in a smooth even layer. Cleaning the spatula often against the side of the bowl will help you spread the frosting smoothly.

Spoon the reserved cinnamon frosting into a small self-sealing freezer bag. Press out the excess air and seal the bag. Cut a tiny hole in one corner of the bag, about 1/16 inch long. Hold the bag about 1/2 inch above a cupcake and slowly pipe 2 circles, one inside the other, on the frosting. Pipe a dot of the frosting in the center. Using a toothpick, and beginning at the center, draw the tip gently through the frosting toward the edge of the cupcake. Move the toothpick about 3/4 inch away and, beginning at the edge of the cupcake, draw it toward the center. Continue pulling shallow lines, alternating the direction of the toothpick, around the top of the cupcake, to form a web pattern. Repeat with the remaining cupcakes.

The cupcakes can be loosely covered and stored at room temperature for up to 3 days.

:: hummingbird swirls ::

Hummingbird Cake is a banana, pecan, and pineapple cake that has a cream cheese frosting. This cupcake version adds the fruit and nuts to a yellow cupcake batter and covers the top of the cupcakes with thick swirls of cream cheese frosting. Frosting cupcakes by piping the frosting through a star-shaped pastry tube is a fast way to add a fancy party finish. Regular or mini, this cupcake works well either way. The batter has a lot of fruit and nuts added to it, so a regular muffin tin produces 12 big-top cupcakes.

Make the cupcakes. Position a rack in the middle of the oven. Preheat the oven to 350°F. Line 12 muffin tin cups with paper cupcake liners or line 4 mini-muffin tins that have 12 cups each with mini–paper liners.

Add the cinnamon, mashed banana, pineapple, and pecans to the cupcake batter and, using an electric mixer on low speed, mix just to blend them together. Fill each regular paper liner with about 1/3 cup of batter, to about 1/4 inch from the top of the liner. Or fill the mini-liners with about 1 1/2 table-spoons batter, to just below the top of the liner.

Bake until the tops are golden and a toothpick inserted in the center comes out clean, about 25 minutes for regular cupcakes or about 16 minutes for mini-cupcakes. Cool the cupcakes for 10 minutes in the pan(s) on a wire rack.

Carefully place the wire rack on top of the cupcakes in their pan (or place one rack on top of one pan of mini-cupcakes). Protecting your hands with pot holders and holding the pan and rack together, invert them to release the cupcakes onto the wire rack. Turn the cupcakes top side up to cool completely. Repeat with the remaining cupcakes if necessary.

Frost the cupcakes. Spoon the frosting into a large pastry bag fitted with a large star tip. Beginning at the edge of each cupcake, pipe swirls of frost-ing to cover the top of each: pipe the frosting in a circular motion or back and forth in swirled lines over the top. Any pattern will look nice. Serve, or cover loosely and refrigerate for up to 3 days.

MAKES 12 BIG-TOP CUPCAKES OR
48 MINI-CUPCAKES

CUPCAKE MAKING :
20 minutes

CUPCAKE BAKING :
350°F. for about 25 minutes
for regular size, or for about
16 minutes for mini-size

CUPCAKES

3/4 teaspoon ground cinnamon

1/2 cup mashed banana (1 banana)

1/2 cup canned crushed pineapple in its own juice, drained

1/2 cup (2 ounces) pecans, finely chopped

Easy-Mix Yellow Cupcake Batter for 12 regular cupcakes (page 23), still in the mixing bowl

FROSTING

1 recipe Cream Cheese Frosting (page 25), at room temperature

::orange-glazed cranberry spice tea cakes::

CUPCAKES

1¼ cups unbleached all-purpose flour

½ teaspoon baking powder

¼ teaspoon baking soda

¼ teaspoon salt

1   teaspoon ground cinnamon

⅛ teaspoon ground nutmeg

2   large eggs

1   cup sugar

½ cup canola or corn oil

1   teaspoon vanilla extract

1   teaspoon grated orange zest

½ cup sour cream

1   cup fresh or defrosted frozen
    cranberries, finely chopped

Cranberries lend a splash of red to these mini-cupcakes. When spread over the warm cupcakes, the orange glaze melts and forms a shiny, translucent topping. These bite-size cupcakes are perfect for serving at a holiday tea party and make a good choice for filling gift tins.

Make the cupcakes. Position a rack in the middle of the oven. Preheat the oven to 350°F. Line 3 mini-muffin tins that have 12 cups each with mini–paper liners. Spray the paper liners with nonstick spray.

Sift the flour, baking powder, baking soda, salt, cinnamon, and nutmeg into a medium bowl and set aside. In a large bowl, using an electric mixer on medium speed, beat the eggs and sugar until the mixture thickens and lightens to a cream color, about 2 minutes. Stop the mixer and scrape the sides of the bowl as needed during mixing. On low speed, mix in the oil, vanilla, and orange zest until blended. Mix in the sour cream until no white streaks remain. Mix in the flour mixture. Mix in the cranberries.

Fill each paper liner with about 1½ tablespoons of batter, to just below the top of the liner. Bake just until the tops feel firm and a toothpick inserted in the center comes out clean, about 16 minutes. Let the cupcakes cool for 5 minutes in the pans on wire racks.

Meanwhile, make the glaze. In a small bowl, whisk the powdered sugar, melted butter, 4 tablespoons of the milk, the orange zest, and vanilla until a smooth, thick, syrupy glaze forms. Add up to 1 tablespoon more milk by the teaspoon if needed to achieve the proper consistency.

Carefully place a wire rack on top of one pan of cupcakes. Protecting your hands with pot holders and holding the pan and rack together, invert them to release the cupcakes onto the wire rack. Turn the cupcakes top side up. Repeat with the remaining cupcakes and glaze them immediately. Use a toothpick to poke 3 or 4 holes in each warm cupcake. Use a small spatula to spread a thin layer of glaze over the top of each cupcake, about 1 teaspoon for each. The glaze will melt on the warm cupcakes and become shiny, and the cupcake tops will show through. Let the cupcakes cool completely. The glaze will become firm.

Arrange 4 pieces of cranberry on top of each cupcake, if desired. Putting the points of the cranberry pieces together in a flower pattern in the center of the cupcake looks nice.

The cupcakes can be covered and stored at room temperature for up to 3 days.

GLAZE

1	cup powdered sugar
3	tablespoons unsalted butter, melted
4	to 5 tablespoons whole milk
1	teaspoon grated orange zest
1/2	teaspoon vanilla extract

~~~~~~~~~~~~~~~~~~~~~~~~~~~~~~~~~~~

| 36 | fresh cranberries, quartered (optional) |

:: white christmas cupcakes ::

MAKES 12 REGULAR CUPCAKES

:::::::::::::::::::::::::::::::::

CUPCAKE MAKING :

35 *minutes*

CUPCAKE BAKING :

350°F, *for about* 20 *minutes*

No snow? No problem. These snow-white cupcakes, with white chocolate frosting and a covering of white chocolate curls dusted with powdered sugar, make any Christmas white.

When making chocolate curls, it is easiest to scrape them from a large, thick piece of chocolate.

Make the cupcakes. Position a rack in the middle of the oven. Preheat the oven to 350°F. Line 12 muffin tin cups with paper cupcake liners.

Sift the cake flour, baking powder, and salt into a medium bowl and set aside. In a small bowl, stir the milk and vanilla and almond extracts together.

In a large bowl, using an electric mixer on medium speed, beat the butter and sugar until smoothly blended and lightened in color, about 3 minutes; the mixture will look sugary and form large clumps. Stop the mixer and scrape the sides of the bowl as needed during mixing. On low speed, add the flour mixture in 3 additions and the milk mixture in 2 additions, beginning and ending with the flour mixture and mixing just until the flour is incorporated and the batter looks smooth. Set aside.

In another large bowl, beat the egg whites with clean beaters on medium speed until foamy, about 30 seconds. Beat on high speed until the egg whites look shiny and smooth and the beaters form lines in the egg whites. If you stop the mixer and lift up the beaters, the whites should cling to the beaters. Stir about one-third of the beaten egg whites into the reserved batter. Use a rubber spatula to fold in the remaining egg whites just until blended.

Fill each paper liner with a scant 1/3 cup of batter, to about 1/4 inch from the top of the liner. Bake just until the tops feel firm and a toothpick inserted in the center comes out clean, about 20 minutes. Cool the cupcakes for 10 minutes in the pan on a wire rack.

Carefully place the wire rack on top of the cupcakes in their pan. Protecting your hands with pot holders and holding the pan and rack together, invert

CUPCAKES

1¼ cups cake flour

¾ teaspoon baking powder

⅛ teaspoon salt

¾ cup whole milk

1 teaspoon vanilla extract

¼ teaspoon pure almond extract

6 tablespoons (¾ stick) unsalted butter, at room temperature

1 cup sugar

3 large egg whites, at room temperature

them to release the cupcakes onto the wire rack. Turn the cupcakes top side up to cool completely.

Make the frosting. Put the white chocolate in a heatproof bowl or the top of a double boiler and place it over, but not touching, a saucepan of barely simmering water (or the bottom of the double boiler). Stir until the chocolate is melted and smooth. Transfer to a large bowl.

Add the butter, cream cheese, and vanilla to the white chocolate and beat with an electric mixer on low speed until smooth and blended, about 1 minute. Add the powdered sugar, mixing until it is incorporated and the frosting is smooth, about 1 minute.

Use a small spatula to spread about 2 tablespoons of frosting on top of each cupcake, mounding it slightly toward the center.

Make the white chocolate curls. Line a baking sheet with wax paper. Hold the white chocolate between the palms of your hands for a minute or two to warm and soften it slightly. Then hold the chocolate in one hand and use a swivel vegetable peeler to scrape curls from the block of chocolate, letting them fall in a single layer onto the baking sheet. Scrape the peeler away from you in 1 1/2- to 2-inch-long strokes along all sides of the white chocolate until you have 2 cups of large curls. You will not use all of the chocolate, but a large piece of chocolate is less likely to crumble and break. If the chocolate curls begin to flake and break, the chocolate is too hard and you should hold it between your hands to briefly soften it again. Put the baking sheet in the freezer for about 30 minutes to firm the curls for easier handling.

Spoon the curls on top of the frosted cupcakes and dust lightly with powdered sugar.

The cupcakes can be covered and stored at room temperature for up to 3 days.

FROSTING

3	ounces white chocolate, chopped
1/4	cup (1/2 stick) unsalted butter, at room temperature
4	ounces cream cheese, at room temperature
1	teaspoon vanilla extract
1 1/2	cups powdered sugar

~~~~~~~~~~~~~~~~~~~~~~~~~~~~~

WHITE CHOCOLATE CURLS

6- to 8-ounce block of white chocolate

~~~~~~~~~~~~~~~~~~~~~~~~~~~~~

Powdered sugar for dusting

:: *spring bouquet cupcakes* ::

MAKES 12 REGULAR CUPCAKES

: :

CUPCAKE MAKING :

30 minutes

CUPCAKE BAKING :

350°F, for about 23 minutes

Cheering graduates, welcoming new babies, showering brides, honoring mothers, or just rejoicing in the end of winter—spring has so many good reasons to celebrate. Decorated with a rainbow of colorful flowers perched on pure white frosting, these cupcakes fit perfectly into any of these celebrations. And no one will ever guess, but the flowers are easily made from gumdrops that are rolled flat and pinched into flower shapes.

Use regular-size (about 1/2-inch) gumdrops to make the flowers. You could also buy premade sugar flowers or press an edible flower into the top of each cupcake. An assortment of sugar flowers can be ordered from New York Cake and Baking Distributors (see Mail-Order Sources, page 141). Pansies, violets, or nasturtiums also makes a gorgeous finish, but be sure to use organic flowers that have not been sprayed.

CUPCAKES

Easy-Mix Yellow Cupcake Batter for 12 regular cupcakes (page 23)

FROSTING

1/2 cup (1 stick) unsalted butter, at room temperature

2 tablespoons vegetable shortening, such as Crisco, at room temperature

1/8 teaspoon salt

2 1/2 cups powdered sugar

5 tablespoons heavy whipping cream

1 teaspoon vanilla extract

1/2 teaspoon almond extract

:: continued

Make the cupcakes. Position a rack in the middle of the oven. Preheat the oven to 350°F. Line 12 muffin tin cups with paper cupcake liners.

Fill each paper liner with a scant 1/4 cup of batter, to about 1/2 inch below the top of the liner. Bake just until the tops feel firm and a toothpick inserted in the center comes out clean, about 23 minutes. Cool the cupcakes for 10 minutes in the pan on a wire rack.

Carefully place the wire rack on top of the cupcakes in their pan. Protecting your hands with pot holders and holding the pan and rack together, invert them to release the cupcakes onto the wire rack. Turn the cupcakes top side up to cool completely.

Make the frosting. In a large bowl, using an electric mixer on low speed, beat the butter, vegetable shortening, and salt to blend them. On low speed, beat in the powdered sugar, cream, and vanilla and almond extracts until smoothly blended, then beat on medium-high speed for 1 minute to lighten the frosting.

:: continued

GUMDROP FLOWERS

Powdered sugar for dusting the rolling surface

24 to 30 gumdrops in assorted colors (no black)

Using a thin metal spatula, spread about 2 tablespoons of frosting evenly over the top of each cupcake. Reserve a teaspoon of frosting to glue the flower centers, if desired. (See the instructions below for different options.)

Make the gumdrop flowers. Dust a rolling surface lightly with powdered sugar. Using a rolling pin, roll about 20 of the gumdrops to flatten them to about 1¼-inch circles. Start by cutting about 24 thin strips from the green gumdrops to use for stems, and use other colors for petals. If desired, for two-toned flowers, cut about 12 thin slices (less than ⅛ inch thick) from some of the remaining gumdrops. Then roll a slice of gumdrop in a contrasting color onto the center of 12 of the flattened gumdrops.

To brighten the color and remove some of the sugar, pat the gumdrops with a damp paper towel. To form the flowers, hold a flattened gumdrop circle with your thumb and two fingers and pinch the center of the bottom to form softly ruffled petals. The sticky gumdrops are quite malleable and can be shaped as you wish. For the gumdrop flowers that are of a single color, cut a small piece of gumdrop in a contrasting color and press it into a tiny (about 1/16 inch or slightly larger) ball, dip the ball in the reserved frosting, and press it, frosting side down, into the center of a gumdrop flower. Arrange 1 or 2 stems on top of each cupcake—a V pattern looks nice for two stems—and place one or two flowers on or around the stems.

The cupcakes can be covered and stored at room temperature for up to 3 days.

CHOICES If using edible fresh flowers (as pictured), arrange them on the cupcakes just before serving them. Store leftover cupcakes in the refrigerator.

Instead of flowers, pastel-colored Necco wafers make a nice spring decoration. Arrange 3 or 4 of the wafers as a border around the edges of each cupcake or in any other pattern that you like.

:: chocolate cupcakes with peppermint icing

When this book was just a great idea that my editor, Amy Treadwell, was brainstorming with me, she asked if I could include a chocolate cupcake with peppermint icing. Definitely yes! The result is these chocolate cupcakes covered with a thick, soft peppermint icing, topped off with the crunch of crushed peppermint candy. Small candy canes or disks of striped peppermint candy could also decorate the tops. These cupcakes measure about 3¼ inches across the top, so there is plenty of space for lots of icing.

Make the cupcakes. Position a rack in the middle of the oven. Preheat the oven to 350°F. Line 12 muffin tin cups with paper cupcake liners.

Fill each paper liner with a generous ⅓ cup of batter, to about ⅛ inch below the top of the liner. Bake just until the tops feel firm and a toothpick inserted in the center comes out clean, about 20 minutes. Cool the cupcakes for 10 minutes in the pan on a wire rack.

Use a small knife to loosen any tops that have stuck to the top of the pan. Carefully place the wire rack on top of the cupcakes in their pan. Protecting your hands with pot holders and holding the pan and rack together, invert them to release the cupcakes onto the wire rack. Turn the cupcakes top side up to cool completely.

Make the icing. Sift the powdered sugar into a large bowl. Heat the butter and water in a small saucepan over medium-low heat until the butter melts. Remove the pan from the heat and stir in the peppermint extract. Pour the warm mixture over the powdered sugar, then whisk vigorously until it is smooth. The icing will be soft but thick enough to cling to the top of the cupcakes.

Use a small spatula to spread a scant 2 tablespoons of icing over the top of each cupcake, spreading it carefully to the edges. Leaving about a ¾-inch plain edge, sprinkle about 2 teaspoons of the crushed peppermint candy over each cupcake.

The cupcakes can be covered and stored at room temperature for up to 3 days.

MAKES 12 BIG-TOP CUPCAKES

CUPCAKE MAKING :
20 minutes

CUPCAKE BAKING :
350°F, for about 20 minutes

CUPCAKES

Chocolate Sour Cream Cupcake Batter for 12 big-top cupcakes (page 24)

ICING

2½ cups powdered sugar

¼ cup (½ stick) unsalted butter

6 tablespoons water

¼ teaspoon peppermint extract

½ cup (3 ounces) crushed peppermint candy

:: celebration cupcakes

:: chocolate sweetheart cupcakes ::

MAKES 12 BIG-TOP CUPCAKES

: :

CUPCAKE MAKING :

20 minutes

CUPCAKE BAKING :

350°F, for about 20 minutes

CUPCAKES

Chocolate Sour Cream Cupcake
Batter for 12 big-top cupcakes
(page 24)

CHOCOLATE HEARTS

6 ounces semisweet chocolate,
chopped

FROSTING

2 cups powdered sugar

1/2 cup (1 stick) unsalted butter,
cut into pieces

1/2 cup granulated sugar

1/2 cup half-and-half

More than any other flavor, chocolate symbolizes Valentine's Day. This chocolate cupcake, with a thick layer of fudge frosting and chocolate heart decoration, is a valentine that is certain to win over your sweetheart.

Although they are quite impressive, chocolate hearts are a cinch to make. You simply spread melted chocolate over parchment paper, let the chocolate sit until it is soft but no longer runny, and cut out hearts with a metal cutter. Using different-size cutters to make an assortment of hearts is a nice touch.

Make the cupcakes. Position a rack in the middle of the oven. Preheat the oven to 350°F. Line 12 muffin tin cups with paper cupcake liners.

Fill each paper liner with a generous 1/3 cup of batter (about 6 tablespoons), to just below the top of the liner. Bake just until the tops feel firm and a toothpick inserted in the center comes out clean, about 20 minutes. Cool the cupcakes for 10 minutes in the pan on a wire rack.

Carefully place the wire rack on top of the cupcakes in their pan. Protecting your hands with pot holders and holding the pan and rack together, invert them to release the cupcakes onto the wire rack. Turn the cupcakes top side up to cool completely.

Make the chocolate hearts. Put the chocolate in a heatproof bowl or the top of a double boiler and place it over, but not touching, a saucepan of barely simmering water (or the bottom of the double boiler). Stir the chocolate until it is melted and smooth. Remove from the water.

Cut a piece of parchment paper to fit the back of a baking sheet and tape the paper to the back of the baking sheet. This gives you a steady, smooth surface for spreading the chocolate. Using a thin metal spatula, spread the melted chocolate evenly over the parchment into a rectangle about 10 by 13 inches. The chocolate should be thick enough so that the paper does not show through the chocolate. The chocolate will look shiny and wet. Put the baking sheet in the refrigerator and chill it just until the chocolate looks dull and dry and is soft but no longer runny, about 3 minutes; do not let the chocolate harden.

Using heart-shaped cookie cutters (cutters that are 2 inches or smaller work well), cut out about 24 small chocolate hearts or 12 large ones, leaving the cutouts on the pan. If the chocolate is too soft and runs back together, chill it until it is firm enough to hold the cut marks. Or if the chocolate hardens and then cracks when it is cut, warm the chocolate sheet in a low oven for a few seconds. Return the marked chocolate sheet to the refrigerator to firm completely, about 30 minutes.

Remove the baking sheet from the refrigerator. Turn the chocolate paper over on the baking sheet and peel the paper from the chocolate. The chocolate should separate easily into heart shapes; use a small knife to separate or trim any hearts that stick. Use a spatula to lift the hearts onto a plate, layering them between wax paper. Cover and refrigerate. (The hearts can be refrigerated for up to 1 week.) The scraps make good snacks.

Make the frosting. Sift the powdered sugar into a large bowl; set aside. In a medium saucepan, combine the butter, granulated sugar, half-and-half, and honey and heat over medium heat, stirring occasionally, until the butter melts and the sugar dissolves; do not let boil. Remove the pan from the heat, add the chopped chocolate, and stir until the chocolate melts. Return the pan to low heat for a minute or so if necessary to melt the chocolate completely.

:: continued

2	tablespoons honey
3	ounces semisweet chocolate, finely chopped
3	ounces unsweetened chocolate, finely chopped
1	teaspoon vanilla extract
1	teaspoon instant coffee, dissolved in 1 teaspoon water

:: celebration cupcakes

Stir the vanilla and dissolved coffee into the chocolate mixture, then pour the warm mixture over the powdered sugar. Using an electric mixer, beat on low speed until the powdered sugar is incorporated and no white specks remain. Press a piece of plastic wrap onto the surface and refrigerate until the frosting is cool to the touch, about 1 hour.

Using the electric mixer on medium speed, beat the frosting until it is smooth, creamy, and slightly lightened in color, about 30 seconds. Using a thin metal spatula, spread about 1/4 cup of frosting evenly over the top of each cupcake. Arrange 1 large chocolate heart or 2 small ones on the frosting on each cupcake. Serve, or cover and refrigerate.

The cupcakes can be refrigerated for up to 3 days. Let sit at room temperature for about 20 minutes before serving.

CHOICES The chocolate shapes can be cut with any cookie cutters to match a holiday or mood. Trees, stars, or shamrocks are all good options. Another idea is to cut out numbers for a birthday celebration.

:: red, white, and blueberry cupcakes ::

Fire up the barbecue, light the sparklers, invite the neighbors. Celebrate Memorial Day and the Fourth of July and graduations, and that there are blueberries and raspberries and blackberries and strawberries in season, sweet and good and dripping with juice. Put the berries with the cupcakes, whip up the cream, and have a great time—it's summer.

Make the cupcakes. Position a rack in the middle of the oven. Preheat the oven to 350°F. Line 12 muffin tin cups with paper cupcake liners.

Put the blueberries in a small bowl and stir them gently with 1 tablespoon of the flour; set aside. Sift the remaining 1 cup plus 3 tablespoons flour, the baking powder, and salt into a medium bowl; set aside.

In a large bowl, using an electric mixer on medium speed, beat the butter and sugar until smoothly blended and lightened in color, about 2 minutes. Stop the mixer and scrape the sides of the bowl as needed during mixing. Beat in the egg whites in 2 additions, mixing until smoothly blended. Add the vanilla and almond extracts and beat for 2 minutes. The batter should look smooth but foamy. On low speed, add half of the flour mixture, mixing just to incorporate it. Mix in the milk. Mix in the remaining flour mixture until it is incorporated and the batter looks smooth. Use a rubber spatula to gently fold the blueberries and raspberries into the batter.

Fill each paper liner with 1/4 cup of batter, to about 1/2 inch below the top of the liner. Bake just until the tops feel firm and a toothpick inserted in the center comes out clean, about 25 minutes. Cool the cupcakes for 10 minutes in the pan on a wire rack.

:: continued

MAKES 12 REGULAR CUPCAKES

CUPCAKE MAKING :
20 minutes

CUPCAKE BAKING :
350°F, for about 25 minutes

CUPCAKES

1/3   cup fresh blueberries

1 1/4   cups unbleached all-purpose flour

1   teaspoon baking powder

1/4   teaspoon salt

1/2   cup (1 stick) unsalted butter, at room temperature

1   cup sugar

4   large egg whites, at room temperature

1   teaspoon vanilla extract

1/2   teaspoon almond extract

1/4   cup whole milk

1/4   cup fresh raspberries

:: continued

:: celebration cupcakes

Carefully place the wire rack on top of the cupcakes in their pan. Protecting your hands with pot holders and holding the pan and rack together, invert them to release the cupcakes onto the wire rack. Turn the cupcakes top side up to cool completely.

Make the topping. In a large bowl, using an electric mixer on medium-high speed, beat the cream, powdered sugar, and vanilla until firm peaks form.

Using a thin metal spatula, spread a generous 3 tablespoons of whipped cream evenly over the top of each cupcake. Gently spoon several raspberries and blueberries over the whipped cream. Refrigerate and serve cold.

The cupcakes can be refrigerated overnight.

TOPPING

2   cups heavy whipping cream

3   tablespoons powdered sugar

1   teaspoon vanilla extract

1/2   cup fresh raspberries

1/3   cup fresh blueberries

:: summer s'more cupcakes ::

MAKES 6 EXTRA-LARGE CUPCAKES

:::::::::::::::::::::::::::::::

CUPCAKE MAKING :
10 minutes

CUPCAKE BAKING :
325°F, for about 20 minutes

2   cups graham cracker crumbs

2   tablespoons sugar

3/4 cup (1½ sticks) unsalted butter, melted

1   cup cut-up milk chocolate candy bars (approximately ½-inch pieces; about 6 ounces)

6   marshmallows

Powdered sugar for dusting

I know why s'mores are so popular: milk chocolate, graham crackers, and melted marshmallows—it makes you want to light the campfire immediately. But there is no need to light a fire for these s'mores. They are as easy as baking a crisp graham cracker crumb and milk chocolate "cupcake" and melting a big marshmallow on top.

Boxes of graham cracker crumbs can be found in the baking section of many supermarkets.

Position a rack in the middle of the oven. Preheat the oven to 325°F. Line 6 extra-large muffin tin cups with large paper cupcake liners. Spray the inside of each liner with nonstick cooking spray.

In a medium bowl, stir the graham cracker crumbs and sugar together. Mix in the melted butter to evenly moisten the crumbs. Mix in the chopped chocolate.

Fill each paper liner with about ½ cup of the crumb mixture, to about ¾ inch below the top of the liner. Press the mixture firmly into the paper liners, making a slight indentation in the center.

Bake for 10 minutes. Remove the pan from the oven and place a marshmallow in the center of each cupcake. Bake for about 10 minutes more, until the marshmallows soften and the tops turn light golden. Cool the cupcakes for 20 minutes in the pan on a wire rack. Then, holding the edges of the paper liners, lift the cupcakes from the pan onto the wire rack to cool completely.

Remove the paper liners from the cooled cupcakes. Dust the tops lightly with powdered sugar and serve.

The cupcakes can be covered and stored at room temperature for up to 3 days.

mail-order sources

UNITED STATES

King Arthur Flour Baker's Catalogue
P. O. Box 876
Norwich, VT 05055
(800) 827-6836
Fax: (800) 343-3002
www.kingarthurflour.com
Baking equipment and ingredients, including
unbleached all-purpose flour, dried fruits,
peeled hazelnuts, and almond paste

New York Cake and Baking Distributors
56 West 22nd Street
New York, NY 10010
(800) 942-2539; (212) 675-2253
Fax: (212) 675-7099
www.nycake.com
Muffin tins; a large assortment of decorating
supplies, including edible royal icing flowers,
many colors and sizes of glitter, sprinkles,
dragees, and other decorations; paper baking
cups in many sizes and colors

Penzeys Spices
P. O. Box 924
193000 West Janacek Court
Brookfield, WI 53008-0924
(800) 741-7787
Fax: (262) 785-7678
www.penzeys.com
Complete selection of fresh spices and extracts;
high-quality extra-fancy Vietnamese cassia
cinnamon.

Williams-Sonoma
100 North Point Street
San Francisco, CA 94133
(800) 541-2233
Fax: (702) 363-2541
www.williams-sonoma.com
Baking equipment and ingredients

AUSTRALIA

Peter's of Kensington
57 Anzac Parade, Kensington
Sydney, AU 2033
61 (0)2 9662 1099
Fax: 61 (0)2 9662 7835
www.petersofkensington.com
Cookware and small kitchen appliances;
gourmet foods

Cookaholics
61 (0)8 8338 2644
Shop 59, Burnside Village
447 Portrush Road, Glenside
Adelaide, AU 5065
Cookware and kitchen equipment

CANADA

Ares Kitchen and Baking Supplies
2355-A Trans-Canada Highway
Pointe-Claire, Quebec
Canada H9R 5Z5
(888) 624-8008; (514) 695-5225
Fax: (514) 695-0756
Baking equipment
www.arescuisine.com

FRANCE

E. Dehillerin
18-20, rue Coquillière
75001 Paris, France
01 42 36 53 13
Fax: 01 42 36 54 80
www.e-dehillerin.fr
Baking equipment

NEW ZEALAND

Briscoes
116 Taranaki Street
Wellington, NZ 6001
64 (0)4 384 4166
Fax: 64 (0)4 384 4648
www.briscoes.co.nz
Cookware and appliances

UNITED KINGDOM

David Mellor
4 Sloane Square
London SW1, England
020 7730 4259
Fax: 020 7730 4259
www.davidmellordesign.com
Kitchen utensils and cookware

Divertimenti
139-141 Fulham Road
London SW3 6SD, England
020 7581 8065
Fax: 020 7823 9429
www.divertimenti.co.uk
Baking equipment, cookware, and small appliances

table of equivalents

The exact equivalents in the following tables have been rounded for convenience.

LIQUID/DRY MEASURES

U.S.	Metric
1/4 teaspoon	1.25 milliliters
1/2 teaspoon	2.5 milliliters
1 teaspoon	5 milliliters
1 tablespoon (3 teaspoons)	15 milliliters
1 fluid ounce (2 tablespoons)	30 milliliters
1/4 cup	60 milliliters
1/3 cup	80 milliliters
1/2 cup	120 milliliters
1 cup	240 milliliters
1 pint (2 cups)	480 milliliters
1 quart (4 cups, 32 ounces)	960 milliliters
1 gallon (4 quarts)	3.84 liters
1 ounce (by weight)	28 grams
1 pound	454 grams
2.2 pounds	1 kilogram

OVEN TEMPERATURE

Fahrenheit	Celsius	Gas
250	120	1/2
275	140	1
300	150	2
325	160	3
350	180	4
375	190	5
400	200	6
425	220	7
450	230	8
475	240	9
500	260	10

LENGTH

U.S.	Metric
1/8 inch	3 millimeters
1/4 inch	6 millimeters
1/2 inch	12 millimeters
1 inch	2.5 centimeters